I WAS
Adopted
TWICE

My Parents' Love,
My Father's Redemption

I WAS *Adopted* TWICE

My Parents' Love, My Father's Redemption

PATRICIA A. DOUGLAS

SWEET PEA PUBLISHING

NASHVILLE

I Was Adopted Twice: My Parents' Love, My Father's Redemption
Published by Sweet Pea Publishing
4183 Franklin Rd. Suite B1#190
Murfreesboro, TN 37128
www.Mapdministries.com

Queries regarding rights and permissions should be addressed to: Sweet Pea Publishing at Sweetpeapublishing27@gmail.com.

ISBN: 978-0-578-82316-4

Interior design by Arlana Johnson

Cover design by The Grace Effect

Photography by Misty Westebbe

While the author has made every effort to provide accurate Internet addresses at the time of publication, neither the publisher nor the author assumes any responsibility for errors or for changes that occur after publication.

20 21 22 23 24 — 9 8 7 6 5 4 3 2 1

Printed in the United States of America

DEDICATION

To my Father God and to my parents,
Leslie and Dahlia Parker, who are now together in heaven
enjoying the Lord.

ACKNOWLEDGMENTS

I want to thank God, the Father of my Lord Jesus Christ, for the opportunity to finally write down on paper what has been in my heart.

I'm very grateful for the natural parents that God chose for me in this earth, Leslie and Dahlia Parker. They were by far the best Mom and Daddy that a child could have. While they were not perfect, they loved God with all their hearts, minds, souls and strength. Thank you for all the love, care, compassion, discipline, godly teaching, training and spiritual guidance over the years. It was an honor for me to be your daughter. My love to you both, forever.

To my husband, Mark. Thank you for being so supportive, not only in the writing of my first book, but in everything I have experienced and stepped out into during our years of marriage. Because of your love for God first, and your spiritual insight, you have helped me to understand so much about who I am.

Thank you to my children Joshua, Marketta and Charles, for your individual demonstrations of support that indeed have been favorable. Even though I haven't been the perfect mom, your love for me has been unconditional.

Special thanks to Arlana Johnson who immediately grasped the vision of this book just with the title alone. With the help and aid of the Holy Spirit, her hard work and perseverance has made this vision become a reality.

To those in my Covenant Circle whom I love and cherish, thank you all.

I cannot possibly write down the names of all of the people who have supported me throughout the years. So, to everyone who has been an important part of my life, thank you!

CONTENTS

Introduction   1

Chapter One   7

Chapter Two   27

Chapter Three   41

Chapter Four   59

Chapter Five   79

Chapter Six   97

Chapter Seven   115

Chapter Eight   137

Chapter Nine   155

Epilogue   175

Prayer of Salvation   183

Notes   185

INTRODUCTION

In writing this book I've had to reach back into the past and grab hold of memories long forgotten, buried deep like treasures hidden in my heart. I have remembered stories about my experiences growing up and becoming a woman, and the wonderful people who have given shape, color and definition to who I am today. I think we all have to do this at some point to better understand who we are, what we were made to do, and how to reach our destination in life.

In all of my reflection over the years, I can clearly point to what I now see as the most significant events in my life. That is, being adopted. Not once, but twice. Now, when I say this a lot of assumptions may run through your mind about what being adopted twice could mean. After all, being adopted once is a big enough deal for most people. It changes your life forever. You can be headed one way, but then a choice made by strangers who want to love you, takes your life in a totally different direction. What happens to you when you are adopted twice? How is that even possible, and how does your life come together? In *I Was Adopted Twice* I want to share what all of this has meant for me.

First, I will start by defining the word "adoption". When most people hear the root word "adopt" they probably know what it means. Basically, it's when someone takes a child in and raises them as their own. According to The Merriam-Webster Dictionary, to adopt means to take by choice into a relationship, to take voluntarily; to choose someone to receive special recognition; to formally approve or accept.

In the 1828 Webster's Dictionary, one of the original editions of the Merriam-Webster, "to adopt" means to take a stranger into one's family, as son and heir; to take one who is not a child, and treat him as one, giving him a title to the privileges and rights of a child.[1] In this sense—spiritually—adoption means to receive the sinful children of men into the invisible church, and into God's favor and protection, by which they become heirs of salvation by Christ Jesus.

There is so much to dig into in these definitions. Let me just highlight a few words that stand out to me:

- *Choose:* to select, especially after consideration; to decide; to have a preference for.
- *Accept:* to receive willingly; to agree to; to assume an obligation to pay.

2

- *Heir:* one who inherits or is entitled to inherit property, rank, title or office.
- *Privilege*: a right or immunity granted as an advantage or favor especially to some and not others.

I can relate each of these terms to both of the times that I was adopted. You see, I was adopted naturally and spiritually. By my parents Leslie and Dahlia Parker and by my heavenly Daddy, Father God. When my parents adopted me, they first chose me and then accepted me as their child. They took me into their home and treated me as an heir, giving me all of the privileges they would have allowed their biological child to have.

Years later, I was adopted by Father God into His Son, Jesus Christ, and His kingdom. Ephesians 1:4-6 says, "According as he hath chosen us in him before the foundation of the world, that we should be holy and without blame before him in love: having predestinated us unto the adoption of children by Jesus Christ to himself, according to the good pleasure of his will, to the praise of the glory of his grace, wherein he hath made us accepted in the beloved." And in Romans 8:16-17 (AMPC), "The Spirit Himself [thus] testifies together with our own spirit, [assuring us] that we are children of God. And if we are [His] children, then we are [His] heirs also: heirs of God and fellow heirs with Christ [sharing His inheritance with Him]; only we must share His suffering if we are to share His glory." There is so much more that the Bible has to say about our adoption by God and I will share more on that later.

Dear reader, you must know that God chose you before the foundation of the world. Before you were knit together in your mother's womb, He knew and predestined you. There is no greater way to be chosen or accepted. There is no inheritance or privilege more valuable than what you receive as a child of God. I was chosen by my adoptive parents, but I had to decide to accept being chosen by the Lord. The same is true for us all. Regardless of our natural upbringing we have the opportunity to receive the Lord Jesus Christ. With that comes assurance, acceptance, everlasting love and the keys to a destiny that was determined for us before we were born.

If you have not made the decision to receive Jesus, I encourage you to do that now (see Prayer of Salvation on page 183).

As you read this book it is my prayer that you will see through my life story, how God can mark us and keep His hand of favor upon us. I hope that you will see how God intricately wove together the details of my existence so that both my natural and spiritual lives have worked together for my good. No experience has been wasted. No mistake has been unsolvable. Every promise of God has been and will be yes and amen. Father God continues to write the story of Patricia Ann Douglas. While He is not finished with me yet, I can look back in awe of what He has accomplished in and through me already. He has planned out every detail so perfectly—for me and for my family. And I know the same is true for you.

CHAPTER ONE

Chosen, Not Abandoned

The headlights of our 1967 Lincoln lit the path ahead as Daddy, Mom and me slowly circled the makeshift dirt parking lot. There were so many cars filing in it was hard to find an empty spot. I don't think I'd ever seen that many people in one place before. Much like today, in the 1960s, summers in the South were intensely hot and the evenings didn't give much relief. Back then many cars didn't have air conditioning, ours included, so we caught whatever breeze we could with the windows rolled down.

We'd arrived early to be sure we got seats for the tent meeting. The service was going to be held on the other side of a large field. In the distance, I could hear the faint sound of musicians warming up. They were off-key at first, just making noise. You know, when each musician is tuning his instrument individually, listening to perfect the pitch. The three of us got out of the car and started walking.

After a few minutes, the musicians came together to produce the beautiful sound of worship. The music drew me. As we got closer, the smell of dirt and grass was replaced by fresh cut wood. We were walking toward what looked like a huge, white umbrella. It was held up by several big poles and tied down with fat ropes, and the biggest nails I'd ever seen. I thought it was very strange and wondered, *will that big thing fold up and fall down on us?*

At the tent's entrance, the ground felt funny. I looked down and saw that we were standing on soft, dusty material that gathered around my feet. It was sawdust, but at five years old I had no idea what it was and I worried that my new, black patent leather Mary Janes would get dirty. In those days, people wore their Sunday best to church and I was not pleased about messing up my shoes. Even now when I think of the tent meetings we attended, I can smell the woodsy scent and see the tiny pieces of chopped wood mixed in with fine shavings.

Church services, no matter where they were held, were a time to be dressed up. Daddy would wear a three-piece suit with a tie and Mom, a jacket and skirt with a lovely blouse that tied in a bow at the neck. She wore stockings back then, the kind that were held in place by garters. Never pantyhose. Like me, she wore black patent leather shoes except that hers were heels. And always, White Shoulders perfume—a delicate blend of gardenia, jasmine and lily of the valley flowers. The fragrance seemed to float around her. She didn't wear much makeup at all, just a little pink lipstick for color.

The three of us had come to attend a service put on by A. A. Allen, one of the most well-known evangelists of that time, and among the first to launch what would now be called a media ministry. He produced a television show and a publication called *Miracle Magazine* to promote the signs, miracles, and wonders that broke out at his meetings. Reverend Allen's Healing Revival Campaigns traveled across the country and attracted tens of thousands of people at a time, including in the South. He was among the few who defied the Jim Crow laws by holding integrated services.

People were packed inside to attend the meeting. I stood close to Daddy and Mom as we worshipped, listened to Rev. Allen preach the Word and witnessed incredible miracles. My eyes were fixed on A. A. Allen as he placed his hand on the head of a sick man. He said some words to him and commanded that he be healed in Jesus' name. Instantly, the man fell backward. Another man caught him and eased him to the ground. My eyes went wide. I was amazed by what I saw.

Grabbing Mom's hand, I pulled gently to bring her ear down to my lips. I whispered, "Mama, that's what I wanna do."

"Do what?" she asked, looking at me.

"Touch people so they fall," I said.

Mom turned to Daddy and asked if he'd heard what I said. He shook his head as if to say, "No" and she repeated what I'd confidently told her.

As children we can never know how our early experiences will affect our lives. When every detail of a day or period of time lines up divinely—putting you in the right place at just the moment you are supposed to be there—it is God's perfect will coming forth. It is His intention to establish us on the unique path He has created for our lives. And so, I had no idea how what I saw and heard at the tent meeting that night, would be just one of many moments that would forever change me.

* * *

I believe I am special because I was adopted. And I think that adoptees are special because they are chosen. People are born into families—not selected by them. There's just something significant about being the one picked out of several other children. I don't say this out of arrogance, but it's the truth. Mom has often shared the story of how she and Daddy chose me to be their daughter. It was in March of 1961. They didn't have any children of their own, and years later I learned that they'd lost a child—a baby boy. At the time of my adoption, my parents were in their late thirties, which was considered to be old for having children. They drove to a foster home in Clarksville, Tennessee to meet the children living there.

When they arrived, Mom saw several children in the room. She approached the crib that I was in, bent down, looked through the bars and saw me. She said that the Holy Spirit quietly told her that I was the one. That has always meant a lot to me because she could've stopped at the crib of any child there. But the Lord had highlighted me.

"She's the one," she told Daddy softly, which was her usual manner of speaking. Mom rarely raised her voice unless the power of God took hold of her.

"Are you sure, Dahlia?" Daddy replied.

"Leslie, yes, I know she is," she said.

I like to think about that moment.

The rules around adoption were very different back then, so that same day the agency allowed Mom and Daddy to take me out for a few hours. The next visit was for an entire week. And then it was decided. I find it incredible that God would place me with them. And that they would know that I was their child. I just think of how intricately God operates— how He planned this thing out. Before He created the world, He said:

Patricia Ann will be born on September 8, 1960 at 7:36 a.m. and put up for adoption. In six months, while she's still in foster care, Leslie and Dahlia Parker will visit on this day, at this time, and they will adopt her.

Thinking about this with our limited, human minds we might believe that's a lot of orchestrating. But to God it wasn't a hard thing at all. Mom told me, there was another couple from Kentucky who was supposed to adopt me. The paperwork had been completed, so I was told, but the adoption fell through. I don't know why. I think about all of that, and I know for sure it just was not God's plan for me to be with any other family.

The day Mom and Daddy brought me home, Mom's parents, Grandma Lena and Grandpa Repps were the first to see me. They lived with my parents at the time. Mom called her sister, my aunt Folia, who lived down the street and told her to come to the house.

"I have something to show you," she said.

Aunt Folia and Uncle Oney came right over, expecting to see a puppy or a new set of furniture. Instead, when they walked in the living room, there I was sitting in the middle of the floor. As my aunt tells it, she ran over and scooped me up into her arms.

"Dahlia, wherever did you get her?" she exclaimed.

My aunt always remarked about how amazed they were to see me.

* * *

Mom and Daddy met at Fort Campbell, a Kentucky military base where Daddy was stationed in the 1940s. Mom worked in the commissary. I can see why he would've been attracted to Mom. She has always been gorgeous, with bright eyes that at times were green, sometimes blue, depending on how the light hit them. I'm sure this intrigued Daddy. At just 4'11" she was petite and the perfect height for his 5'4" frame. In addition to being soft-spoken, she was compassionate and spunky.

Daddy was very handsome. I don't remember him having hair while I was growing up, but I know from pictures that he did in his younger days. While he wasn't a tall man, he had a strong presence, and commanded respect. The two married in 1948 at the army base. While he was enlisted, they traveled overseas to Germany, Australia and Italy. They were married for 62 years and were very caring and tender toward one another.

My parents were a team, with each of them having their roles: Daddy led our family and provided, and Mom was my primary caretaker and managed the household. Both loved the Lord—my upbringing was deeply rooted in the things of God. As I would come to learn, both Mom and Daddy each had a powerful spiritual mantle that the Father intended for them to carry.

Growing up, I felt dearly loved. Being the only child, some would expect me to have been spoiled, which wasn't true because I didn't always get everything I wanted. I was disciplined. Daddy was very stern, and he believed in whippings. Mom was more lenient, but she would become stricter if she had to repeat herself more than once. She would get after me too, but with switches. As a child, I received an abundance of what I needed, and that was correction and unconditional love.

When I was little, I loved to wear pretty dresses and shiny shoes, complete with a hat, gloves and purse. My mom kept me dressed in dainty clothes that Aunt Folia would sometimes make for me. One of my favorite pictures is of me, Mom, and Aunt Folia sitting in a chair in our yard. I was adorned in my very best. Aunt Folia loved to shop and often would take me downtown with her. Sometimes though, I couldn't go because I was routinely sick with asthma.

When the asthma would flare up, everything in the house would stop. Mom wouldn't allow me to do anything but stay in bed, and she would watch me constantly. Daddy would hover around, coming in my room to check on me from time to time. Once Daddy was getting ready to head out for work, putting on his coat and hat. I stopped him.

"Daddy," I wheezed, my voice raspy and soft. He turned to look at me.

"I don't feel good. Would you sit with me?"

He took off his hat, and with his coat still on, he picked

me up and rocked me in our rocking chair for what seemed like hours.

The asthma would usually act up in the winter, and even if I wasn't having an attack, Mom would layer me in thick, heavy clothing to prevent one from coming on. Wearing all of that clothing actually made breathing that much harder. I attended a Catholic school, and when I arrived in the morning my teacher, who was a nun, would have to peel off my layers: hat, mittens, galoshes, coat and several sweaters, so I could start my day.

As my parents grew in their faith and learned more about the power of the Holy Ghost and signs, wonders and miracles, they approached my illness differently. When an asthma attack would come, they would immediately lay hands on me and pray. Isaiah, a young man who lived down the street, would sometimes join us. Grandma Lena would tell him, "You're going to be a prophet." At the time he wasn't born again or even attending church, and my grandmother began to witness to him. Eventually he accepted Jesus and was filled with the Holy Ghost, with the evidence of speaking in tongues. It seemed like overnight, Isaiah was on fire for the Lord and began to walk in the very anointing my grandmother had prophesied. After that, whenever I was having an attack Mom would always call Isaiah over so that he could join them in agreement for my healing.

Between breaths, I'd whisper, "I'm...gonna marry...Isaiah...Mama."

She'd laugh and say, "Honey, he is too old for you!"

I was six and he was about twenty, but at that age I didn't know any better. Eventually, Isaiah ended up fully walking in his prophetic call, just as my grandmother declared, and traveled the world teaching and preaching. And after a few years, the Lord healed me from the asthma and I was never afflicted by it again.

* * *

Mom and Aunt Folia had two more sisters. The oldest, Aunt Ernestine (Tina), lived in California and third in line, Aunt Permatis (Pat), lived in Kentucky. Aunt Folia was the second born and Mom was the baby.

Mom and her sisters were raised in the country, on a farm in Clarksville, Tennessee. Their family had inherited the land from restitution made to ex-slaves in the 1860s called "40 Acres and a Mule." This was a promise to reward freed slaves for their service as the Civil War ended. From history we know the decision to grant this land was not honored and many blacks ended up becoming sharecroppers, where they worked the land owned by whites and shared the crops at the end of the season. In my family's case, they owned their land outright.

Growing up, the girls had to learn to take up for one another because they were teased a lot for their looks. As they matured, some said that all four of them looked like they could be in Hollywood. But in those days if you were black and there was any ambiguity about your race—if you were very fair and had eyes that were anything other than dark brown—you could become a target. It is well known within African American culture that you could have parents who are obviously black, but you could look like you were mixed with "something." Sometimes it's a recessive gene that pulls from white ancestors to lighten one's skin tone or eye color, and sometimes one's parents might be mixed themselves.

In my mom and aunts' case, their parents were both of mixed race. Grandma Lena was Native American and black and her husband, Grandpa Repps, was half white, or "mulatto." Their daughters were very pretty from the time they were small and because of that they were picked on all of the time. I think that's what made each of them feisty and unafraid of challenge, despite their small statures. They had to be tough, so they would not be pushed around—especially Pat. She was the roughest of the four of them. My mom received the most protection as the baby, but she could and would defend herself if it came to it.

Over time, each of the sisters married and moved on to other parts of the state and country. Pat and Folia never had children. Aunt Tina was the only other sister to have a biological child, my cousin Sandra. She was murdered in 1981 at age twenty-nine, leaving behind small children, and me as the remaining Batson grandchild and niece. I was twenty-one when we received word of my cousin's passing. Aunt Tina was very private, so she didn't tell us about it right away. After a month had passed, she called to tell us that Sandra had been in a car wreck and died. For whatever reason, that just didn't sound right to me. Aunt Folia said that the night before we got the phone call, she'd dreamt about blood.

Eventually Aunt Tina told us the truth. Two police officers on patrol came upon a car parked on the side of a deserted road. The car appeared as if it hadn't been moved for some time. Approaching the vehicle, the officers picked up a stench. They found what was left of my cousin; she'd been killed and stuffed into the trunk. The officers guessed she'd been there about three weeks. Aunt Tina received a phone call and was asked to go to the coroner's office to identify her only child through dental records. My uncle never believed in letting my aunt drive, so she didn't even know how. Still, she found a way to the morgue to make a positive identification, and eventually made arrangements to have Sandra's body cremated. My uncle had passed on by then, so she did all of that by herself. Mom and Daddy flew out to California right after we found out. The police said that they could not even begin to find out who killed Sandra, because murders were so frequent in the area. So that's how it was left.

My family really loved Sandra. They loved us both, and now she was gone. The last time I had seen her was when I was about sixteen. At the end of our visit, she told me she didn't think she was going to see me again.

"Oh, yes you will," I said.

"I don't think so, Patricia," she responded.

Five years later, sure enough, she was dead.

Of course, after her passing I thought back on that last conversation that we'd had. Could she possibly have known something would happen to her? This was a question I wouldn't dare ask aloud. My parents, aunts, and uncles were of an era where you didn't talk about such things. It was tragic and very sad, but it just wasn't something to be discussed.

* * *

Daddy was the first born of three brothers and a sister. They grew up poor, as farmers in Gatesville, North Carolina, and learned to work hard at an early age. They had to do chores in the field before heading out on the two-mile walk to school each morning, sometimes with no shoes. Daddy told me that when he was a boy, he vowed that he would never again live any place where he'd have to walk. He always told the story like this, "When I was a boy, I decided then and there that when I was grown, I would own three cars of my own at one time." And he did.

Daddy and his siblings experienced their share of tragedy when they were young. Their mother died unexpectedly at a young age. Their father was so grieved that he died of a broken heart just over a month later. Their sister also died when she was a very young woman. She had three children: twins and a daughter who lived with us a short while when I was little. With all of that death in the family, it seems that my uncles got caught up in a cycle of grief. I'm not sure they ever recovered from it. Both of them died in their forties, well before my dad, leaving more than a dozen grown children— my cousins—behind.

Daddy pushed himself to make a good life for us. He worked hard, set ambitious goals, and knew how to manage his money well. He did not believe in debt and he was disciplined at saving. He always had several income streams. He retired from the U. S. Army as a highly decorated master sergeant, became a dialysis technician and trainer at the V. A. hospital in Nashville, and sold real estate on the side.

Over the years, Daddy told me stories about fighting in World War II and the Korean War. He never shared many details; I imagine that would have been too painful for him. He did tell me that during his time in combat many soldiers died around him, some were right at his side. "But God kept me," he'd say. Active shells would fall right next to him and not explode; he was never harmed.

One time though, a shell landed in the fox hole that he

was posted in, and before he could react it exploded, throwing him up in the air. He hit the ground hard. When he came to, he realized that everyone around him had been killed.

Daddy retired just before the Vietnam War started. I have a picture of him as a young recruit, and in the photo all of the soldiers were looking directly at the camera, except one. Daddy was gazing at something out of the camera's view, seemingly distracted. Looking at that picture with him one day, I asked why he was the only one looking to the side.

He said, "You know, just as they were taking that picture a bird flew by. I saw it land real close. They took the picture right as I was staring at that little bird."

***

Beyond cousin Sandra's tragic death, I have vivid memories of my oldest aunt. Aunt Tina and her husband, Uncle Larry, relocated to Los Angeles from Tennessee in the 1930s, after they married. For years on Valentine's Day, my birthday, or Christmas she would send me a red dress. It was always lovely, always red. Aunt Tina knew that I loved to dress up in frilly clothes, so she knew exactly what I liked. She also would send me cards, but not the kind I was used to receiving. Each one had a picture of a little black girl dressed charmingly for the occasion, in sweet poses. In the 1960s, finding blacks represented anywhere, let alone on greeting cards, was very unusual. I don't know where in the world she got them, but every year I received at least one in the mail, and every year I looked forward to receiving a package from her.

Aunt Tina was so beautiful. She had darker skin than her sisters, an olive complexion, and had long, dark, wavy hair. She was about 5'2". She looked Hawaiian to me, like the hula dancers I'd seen on TV. I didn't get to see her much because of the distance, but every now and then she and Uncle Larry would come to visit.

My aunt believed strongly in stability. She often would remind me that she worked for Howard Hughes for 45 years building airplanes—starting when she was about eighteen. While she never intentionally tried to pass for white, when she was hired her supervisor definitely thought she was. It wasn't until later in her career that she realized her employee file did not list her as black. Loved and highly respected at her job, Aunt Tina's co-workers never knew her true ethnicity.

My aunt was what I call born-again in a "special way." She was straightforward, no nonsense, and so that meant she was likely to say whatever was on her mind. Her words were unfiltered. And I think it was because after she'd retired, and her husband died, she was forced to become independent. She was a petite woman, and she didn't play. Otherwise people would try to take advantage of her.

One summer, when I was about fifteen, me, Daddy, Mom, Aunt Folia and Uncle Oney flew out to L.A. to visit her. She was on the patio grilling steaks for dinner. When they were done, she went inside to finish preparing our meal. While she was in the kitchen some men came into the yard and told Uncle Oney that they were there to pick up the patio furniture. My uncle told the them to wait there and went in to get my aunt. She went out and confronted the visitors, butcher knife in hand, and let them know that they were two days early and needed to leave. I'll just say she used some language that I cannot include here. I stood, mouth open, and watched my itty-bitty aunt tell off several men twice her size while she waved the knife in her hand to emphasize her point. In the next moment the men had left.

Despite her toughness, Aunt Tina was very gentle and wise. In 1991, when I was about thirty years old, the Lord told me to fly out and spend a week with her. After I arrived at the airport, I caught a taxi to her house. Every morning she fixed me breakfast in her well-seasoned black, cast iron skillet, and asked my requests for lunch and dinner. I told her she didn't have to do that for me, but she said she didn't mind. I'm so glad we spent that time together because it was just two years later that she went home to be with the Lord.

* * *

Since Aunt Pat lived in Kentucky, we would see her several times a year, often driving up to visit. When A. A. Allen and other evangelists of that time would host meetings at the colosseum near where she lived, she'd sometimes attend with us. She had a saying, "We didn't come to stay, we're just passing through." In other words, our time on this earth is brief and our ultimate home is in eternity with the Heavenly Father. Aunt Pat was as comical as she was beautiful, and she had striking green eyes. Out of the sisters, she looked the most like their father. Mom and Aunt Pat had a special bond. Daddy said that they used to be party buddies before they got saved.

As an older woman, Aunt Pat didn't have any teeth and she didn't care. So, every time she talked the words hissed and whistled as they left her mouth. When my daughter, Marketta, was in middle school she had a crush on the boy who lived across the street. One day he happened to be outside.

Aunt Pat whistled, "Ketta, John John is outside." Aunt Pat didn't move fast, but she did that day. She put her cane down, stood up and opened the front door.

"John John, come on over here. Marketta's here," she called out to him.

"Yes ma'am," he said as he strolled across the street.

When John John arrived at the stoop, Marketta said shyly, "Hi, John John…" She still laughs about that today.

Even though Aunt Pat didn't go very far in her education, she encouraged my oldest son, Joshua David, to pursue his. She was a big influence in pushing him to finish school. When he graduated she made sure that she was at the ceremony. She told him that he had to get his diploma. All of my children have very fond memories of Aunt Pat.

After I was grown, married and living in Atlanta, Aunt Tina and Aunt Pat who were widowed, decided to move back to Nashville. Mom found a condo for sale with two suites in it. Mama called the realtors and set everything up so that Tina and Pat could move in, each with their own space. That same year, Aunt Folia and Uncle Oney had purchased a house down the street from Mom and Daddy. So, for two years, until Aunt Tina became the first to pass on, all four sisters lived within walking distance of each other. When they'd get together, which was often, they would marvel at how they were able to all be together again at their ages. They never thought it was possible that they all would be in the same city again. When I would come up to visit it was wonderful, just being with the Golden Girls, as I called them. For a time, I had all my aunts and my Mom with me.

Reflection

I was adopted naturally when my parents chose me out of that group of children at the foster home in Clarksville. With the adoption came my acceptance into a beautiful and colorful family and legacy. Just as I was adopted by my parents, the Bible tells of the natural adoption of Esther by her uncle

Mordecai. Esther 2:7 says, "And he brought up Hadassah, that is, Esther, his uncle's daughter: for she had neither father nor mother, and the maid was fair and beautiful; whom Mordecai, when her father and mother were dead, *took for his own daughter*" (empasis added).

In the last line of this scripture the word *took* is so important. Mordecai took Esther for his own daughter. In other words, he accepted ownership and full responsibility for Esther, which are important aspects of a natural adoption. Mordecai provided her with wisdom to make good decisions, and he nurtured and loved her. He walked alongside Esther during her journey to become the most highly favored queen of that time, and the person chosen by God to save her people. That is powerful!

There are two important points here. The first is to know that a little girl who became an orphan, was adopted and changed the lives of an entire nation. In the same way, my parents adopted me, and my family loved and nurtured me, preparing me to fulfill the destiny that I am living out today.

CHAPTER TWO

Putting Down Roots

I am a daddy's girl. I was grown before I knew how to describe the relationship I had with my Daddy. He was "old school"—not very affectionate and he didn't say the words "I love you" often, but he showed love by providing for me. Yet and still, we were bonded together by heart and spirit from the beginning. And it stayed that way. It's as if the Holy Spirit had given him instructions for how to love me, and at the same time gave me permission to receive every bit of the love he poured out.

As much as my parents had picked me to be their daughter, I know that God chose Dahlia Parker to be my mom and Leslie Mitchell Parker to be my dad. It is the Heavenly Father's design that our earthly fathers are to serve in the flesh as a model of Him. Our dads are supposed to reflect God's nature to their children as protectors, providers and the ones who give them identity. A father is supposed to give us the first tangible example of the Father's unconditional love. Growing up there was no way I could have known what an awesome reflection of God that my dad was, and the eternal impression he would have on me. That is something that I do not take for granted.

I wasn't the only one who benefitted from Daddy's godly character. My daddy stood tall among men. People in our community, church and those he did business with respected him highly. They often sought out his wisdom and counsel. Daddy was steady, responsible and an excellent provider. A visionary, he was in many ways, ahead of his time for a black man living in the South during the pre-Civil Rights era. A man of his word, he could be firm yet gentle. His family adored him—me and Mom, her parents and sisters, and all of my cousins. And he loved all of us dearly. It's from Daddy that I learned how to be wise in business and finances. By example, he taught me to think things through and not to be quick to speak. He also had a sense of humor, and his laughter would fill up a room. And there were two things he did not like—liars and thieves. He would say that you can never trust either one of them. These were all things he taught that remain with me.

* * *

From the time my parents brought me home until I was about four, we lived in Clarksville. Mom's parents had sold their farm years before and purchased another home where they lived until they got up in age. They moved in with Mom and Daddy after that. Around 1964 we all moved to 702 Hart Street in East Nashville, where my earliest memories were made. It was a modest, one story house with pale green wood siding and dark green shutters. I believe it was built in the early 1900s as a single-family home, but had been split into two smaller living spaces, each with its own entrance off of the front porch. Me, Mom and Daddy lived on one side and my grandparents lived on the other. There was a kitchen in the middle that we all shared, and we usually had supper together every evening. The living room had pocket doors that we could pull shut in the evenings for privacy.

My most vivid memories in that house are of the holidays. We had the best Christmases, back when winters were actually winters. Even though we lived in the South, we did have snow, and it would be so cold outside. Decorating was the best time. I watched as Daddy dragged the old wooden ladder out from the garage and propped it against the front of the house. I remember him pulling out the plastic, light-up Santa Claus and tying a rope around its neck. He would ease up the ladder, one rung at a time, slowly pulling old Santa up with him. For the next few weeks, Santa would have the best view in the neighborhood from the top of the house.

Daddy also strung the lights around the edge of the roof. At night, the colored lights were so pretty, and they'd twinkle when the wind blew. Mom would decorate inside. Every year we had a fresh cedar tree and the sweet, evergreen smell would fill the house for days. Mom would hang the ornaments and drape garland, and I would help.

On Christmas Eve I would fall asleep to hearing Mom and Daddy's voices, thinking about the gifts Santa Claus was going to bring me. Early on Christmas morning Mom would call Aunt Folia and Uncle Oney to let them know I was awake and to come on over. We'd all spend the day together. Uncle Oney, the family photographer, would bring his Polaroid camera to capture memories of the day. The most memorable gift that I received when we lived in that house was a little toy piano that I could actually sit at and play. Some years later Mom bought me a real upright piano, which I took lessons for and learned to play. That nurtured my love of music, and I still own that piano to this day.

With my grandparents living right next door, I had a special relationship with my Grandma Lena. She was a gentle soul who loved the Lord, and I remember that she was a praying woman. We would often walk to the A&P grocery store. One day, on our way back home we stopped to sit on a park bench. Grandma Lena let me eat a whole box of Eskimo Pies and then sent me back to the store by myself to buy another box. Another time, when I was about eight years old, my grandmother was helping me bathe. In the middle of my bath, she started crying and saying, "Thank you, Jesus," over and over again. My Grandpa Repps couldn't pronounce my name so he nicknamed me Picka Parker. He walked with a cane that looked like a shepherd's staff. He'd use the crook of that cane to catch me if I was being mischievous. Grandpa Repps passed away in 1965 and Grandma Lena went to be with the Lord in 1971.

* * *

Daddy was flipping houses to make money in the 1960s and 1970s, before it became popular. He was a pioneer in that sense. While we were still living on Hart Street, he had begun to scout out land in other parts of the city. He'd always wanted to design and build his own home and because he was already very involved in the local real estate market, he knew where to make the best investment. He finally settled on two plots in North Nashville. What drew him to the area was the opportunity to spread out and to provide a better education for me.

The land that Daddy decided to buy was far from where we were living both in distance and demographics. It was rural so there were not many homes in the area, and the few houses that had been built there sat on massive plots of land. Also, while our first neighborhood was made up of mostly working-class people, our new one was populated mostly by professionals. Our new street's name, Enchanted

Circle, seemed to say that we were destined to have a good life there. Daddy would always take me with him to check on the progress of the house construction. One day, we stopped by and he found a problem.

"Something's not right," he said.

He looked at the cement slabs that had been poured and were already setting. He walked around the wooden stakes marking where walls would eventually stand. He stopped and looked, walked a little further, stopped and looked again. He crossed his arms and shook his head.

Standing next to him, I looked up and asked, "What's wrong, Daddy?"

"Foundation's too high," he said, turning to walk back toward the car. A few minutes later we were at the offices of Hardaway Construction.

"Leslie, we can't fix that now," said Mr. Hardaway. "Looks like you're gonna have two mother-in-law suites," the contractor told him.

And that's what the house ended up having. Daddy originally designed the house as 3-bedroom, 2-bath house, with a simple basement. But because the foundation was higher than expected, the house ended up having two mother-in-law suites. Grandma Lena lived with us on the main floor; since she was in her eighties she couldn't be on her own. But there was still a full suite with three more bedrooms downstairs.

We moved into the house in September 1968. It sat on an acre and a half of land. Mom loved flowers, and she and Daddy both enjoyed gardening, so he created a very large plot in back of the house. I always remember Daddy smelling one of two ways: either clean, like soap, or like the garden because he was always out there, tilling the dirt, pulling weeds, or picking fruit and vegetables. I liked going to the garden and feed store with Daddy. That's where we would get all the seeds to plant for the garden, and any tools or machines he needed. I remember the smell of that place; it was a mix of soil, seedlings and fertilizer. Daddy taught me how to pick the vegetables we would plant by looking at the pictures on the small seed packets. The first time he showed me, I was confused.

"Daddy, how does a big, ole plant fit in this little bitty package?" I asked, truly not understanding how this could be.

"No, Patricia," Daddy replied. "The pictures show what the plants will look like eventually. They start out as tiny little seeds. We have to plant the seeds and care for them. Then they will grow up to look just like what you see in the pictures."

Planting season was a family affair. All three of us, me, Mom and Daddy, would spend a whole day out in that garden preparing soil and planting seeds. Daddy would till the beds, and Mom would plant the seeds, and cover them with dirt. There was a rhythm to how they worked, dig, drop, cover... dig, drop, cover. And even though we'd spend most of the day outside, the time went by fast. Once the planting was done, my job was to take the empty seed packets, attach them to sticks and push the ends down into the soil to mark off each row. Daddy had explained that the pictures would help us to identify what we had planted, what to look for, and remind us how to care for the seedlings as they grew. Sure enough, over time our plants looked just like the pictures. During our first few harvest seasons I was amazed at the bounty we'd reap from sowing those little seeds. It was like a miracle.

Our garden had every vegetable known to man. We never had to shop at the grocery store for vegetables—or fruit for that matter. We had peach, apple and pecan trees, and grape vines. We planted watermelon and cantaloupe. Many of daddy's dialysis patients had farms with cows and chickens so we always had fresh meat.

The backyard was a place of peace and love in our home. It brought us together. We worked really hard there; mostly Daddy, but me and Mom, too. They could stay in that garden all day. While I enjoyed it, I was not built for the outdoors. As I grew older, I had little interest in gardening anymore and I really didn't like harvesting. But Daddy made me do my part. He would say,

"Patricia, you want to eat?"

"Yes!" I'd say excitedly.

"Then you're gonna go into that garden and pick those black-eyed peas," he'd say.

I'd stomp out to the garden, well at least I imagined I was stomping, fussing under my breath the whole time I was picking those peas.

Once, when I was about ten, I challenged Daddy to a race in the yard.

"I know I can beat you," I called to him, thinking he was far too old to be able to keep up with me. I was growing taller, my legs were getting longer, and I just knew I would win.

"Come on, then," he said. Daddy was wearing black boots, with his green fatigues. I figured he wouldn't be able to keep up in those old army clothes.

I started the count. "On your mark, get set..." by the time I yelled "go!" Daddy was at the other end of the yard. It was as if he was shot out of a cannon.

For my entire childhood, the yard and open lot next door was my play space. A huge rock and some trees, placed just in the right spots, served as markers for my makeshift playhouse. I had a kitchen, living room, bedroom and bathroom all plotted out. I often played by myself. Being an only child, I'd grown used to that and I was perfectly content playing house and pretending I was each member of a family. Daddy left the plot next door empty for almost thirty years before building another house on the land.

Reflection

After being adopted, I was blessed with a wonderful natural father. Before Daddy and Mom adopted me, though, I was an orphan. Those who are without a heavenly Father are orphans, too—in the spirit. Jesus Christ recognized this, so He took us in and called us His own. While we were yet sinners, He gave His life for us, so that we could be called the children of God (see Romans 5:8). That's love!

After taking us in as His own children, there are three things Father God uses to provide clarity and understanding to us: the seed, the Word and the mirror. Just like the pictures on garden seed packets show what the harvest will look like, God's Word is seed, and it mirrors what *we* should look like. James 1:23 says, "For if any be a hearer of the word, and not a doer, he is like unto a man beholding his natural face in a glass: For he beholdeth himself, and goeth his way, and straightway forgetteth what manner of man he was. But whoso looketh into the perfect law of liberty, and continueth therein, he being not a forgetful hearer, but a doer of the work, this man shall be blessed in his deed." The Father's Word gets into us, and with time and watering we eventually get a harvest. That's how we fully walk in sonship and are adopted into the Body.

In the spirit realm we are already sons, we start off as an heir. But due to our sin nature, being born into iniquity it often takes time for us to come into the full realization of who we are. Only the Word of God can bring us into fullness or completeness in Him. Remember we walk by faith and not by sight (2 Corinthians 5:7). So therefore, according to Colossians 2:10, we are already complete in Jesus Christ, it is our thinking that needs to align with what God has said.

Daddy's Army portrait

Mom

Me, age 5 (1965)

CHAPTER THREE

Class With a Little Sass

My Aunt Folia would have been the best mother. There was just something about her. I think she was built to be a nurturer both physically and otherwise. She was petite like her sisters, but heavy-busted. When I needed comforting, I could just lay my head on her bosom and feel safe. My Aunt Folia was my babysitter when Mom and Daddy went out. Uncle Oney had a good job as a secretary clerk for the State of Tennessee, and at the end of each workday he would call my aunt to ask if she needed anything. If I was there, he'd ask after me, too. My response was always M&Ms and he never failed to bring some home when I asked.

I got to spend a lot of time with my aunt growing up. Aunt Folia was a perfect housewife and took good care of my uncle. She prepared fresh meals for him every day, hung her wash on the clothesline in the yard, ironed the sheets and pillowcases and never complained. My uncle was good with gardening and they had a plot in the back yard. It was nowhere near the size of Mom and Daddy's, but it was nice. Aunt Folia and I would take the bus to do our shopping in downtown Nashville and we always dressed up. I was very chatty back then, and people riding the bus or shopping in the store or wherever we were would marvel at how much and how well I spoke. They'd say to Aunt Folia, "Where did you get her?" Aunt Folia would say proudly, "Oh, she's my niece." My aunt told me that people would always say that there was something remarkable about me. It was as if she wanted me to know that people thought I was special. I've always held onto the memories of her saying that.

After arriving downtown, we'd go to Woolworth's on Fifth Avenue, the same Woolworth's where, several years earlier, African American college students staged a series of sit-ins to protest the decades-old practice of segregated lunch counters. The late congressman, John Lewis, who marched with Dr. Martin Luther King Jr., and was arrested almost fifty times, was first arrested during these sit-ins. The Woolworth's still stands to this day and for its part in the Civil Rights movement, it is a registered historic site as part of the Fifth Avenue Historic District in Nashville.[3] It's amazing to me that I have a personal connection to a building that is such an important part of our history.

By the time Aunt Folia and I visited, the lunch counters had long since desegregated. We would eat lunch and she'd order me little hamburgers that were the size of an adult's palm. I would always ask for a large hamburger, but she would rarely order me one. The one time that she did, I didn't finish it. "See, your eyes were bigger than your belly," she said.

After lunch, we'd take our time browsing the aisles there, and at other major department stores at that time, including Castner Knott and Cain-Sloan. I'd always come back home with a special treat from Aunt Folia—an outfit or a toy that I'd picked out.

One day, my aunt had taken a solo shopping trip and afterward she came over to our house. I was sitting at the kitchen table drawing pictures while Mom stood at the stove preparing dinner. Aunt Folia placed her bags on the floor and took a seat, sighing as if she was worn out from the day's errands. She looked over at me, gazing for a bit. Then she rested her chin in her hand and smiled.

"You know, Dahlia, she's going to be very fashionable," she said. "You just watch."

"What do you mean?" Mom said, turning to respond to her. She smoothed her apron.

"I mean she's going to like to dress. She's going to like fashion. That's all."

Aunt Folia looked over at me and smiled. I looked at her and returned the smile. Inside I felt happy because it was as if my aunt was saying I was going to be like her. I really liked the thought of that. And somehow, I think she was happy about it, too.

Aunt Folia was one of the classiest women that I knew. When she wasn't shopping downtown, she would shop from home. Of course, back then online shopping didn't exist; the closest thing to that was ordering by phone via a catalog. Aunt Folia would often receive packages mailed to her from Spiegel or Sears, and sometimes I was at her house when they arrived. She wore Chanel No. 5 and the most beautiful clothes. Although she had a lot of fine things—jewelry, hats, shoes, purses, coats, you name it—she never spent too much. Aunt Folia always managed her money well. I looked up to her and loved to see her in her element. When she was going out, Aunt Folia would wear a lovely dress with high-heeled shoes and a matching hat and purse.

On Sundays, my aunt would wear her fox stole to church. Back then, the fur wraps women wore still had the animal's head, feet and tail attached. Of course, that would never be tolerated today, as the animal rights activists would be up in arms.

One Sunday, I was visiting Aunt Folia's church. As I sat on the pew, right next to her, I felt as if someone was staring at me. I turned to look and our eyes locked. That sly fox of hers was glaring at me with its glassy, unmoving eyeballs. I narrowed my eyes. Whack! I gave Mr. Fox a pop. I tried to turn away and pay attention to what the pastor was saying, but I couldn't focus. Those beady eyes were fixed on me. I stole another look, and sure enough that ugly critter had the nerve to still be staring at me. Whack! I popped him really good that time. Aunt Folia looked over at me, as if to say *child, what in the world are you doing?*

"Well, it's looking at me!" I said to her in a loud whisper. She shushed me and told me to pay attention to the service.

Aunt Folia taught Sunday school and all of the kids loved having her as a teacher, including me when I visited. Of course, she was Mrs. Harris to them, and they would circle around her with questions or wanting attention, "Mrs. Harris this, and Mrs. Harris that." But I was the special one because I had the privilege of having her as my auntie. She was so good with children. Years later, when I was grown, I asked Aunt Folia why she didn't have kids.

"Well, it must not have been in God's plan," she said. "It's not like I didn't do what you do to get them."

We had a good laugh at that. All of my aunts, Mom included, were quick witted and just said things straight. Sometimes they'd make you burst out laughing and sometimes it would make you cringe. Aunt Folia later confided to me that she never even got pregnant. She said it just never happened. Hearing that, my heart ached for her. It was clear to me that she had desired children for a very long time.

***

Every place we lived, Aunt Folia and Uncle Oney lived down the street from us. Both in Clarksville and Nashville. My uncle was 6'3" and it seemed like Aunt Folia barely passed his waist. He towered over the rest of our family. They were married more than sixty years, and their marriage lasted the longest after Mom and Daddy's. Uncle Oney was very good to my aunt and loved her dearly. But they likely wouldn't have ever gotten married, had it been up to his family.

Uncle Oney had a brother, Robert, and they were the only two children their parents had. His family was mixed race, much like Aunt Folia and Mom's. And much like their family, his people experienced their share of tragedy.

Uncle Oney and his brother both served in the army. Robert was heading home on break after being stationed for a period of time. During a brief stop, a man approached him from behind as he stood on the train platform waiting to re-board. The man stabbed Robert, puncturing his lung, killing him. The man was arrested on the spot and jailed for murder. Uncle Oney's family was devastated. They eventually had the opportunity to ask his brother's murderer why he'd done it. The man said he didn't really know, but as it turned out, he was on the train with Robert and some other young ladies. The women struck up a conversation with Robert and flirted with him, making the man jealous, so he stabbed him.

After Robert was killed, Uncle Oney was discharged from the service. Because of the army's sole survivor rule that says if one son had been killed while serving, they wouldn't allow the remaining son to stay in service. Both sons were very close to their parents and after Robert died, Uncle Oney's mother clung very closely to him.

The reason behind the resistance to Uncle Oney and Aunt Folia marrying was due to his family's social status. Everyone in Uncle Oney's family a generation back was educated, and they were all professionals. Mom and her sisters were not. My uncle's mother was a schoolteacher, and she wanted her son to marry someone of a similar "class". Their family had jobs that required higher levels of education than most; at that time, they were referred to as "high society" black people. Back then, just as you may find today, people of a similar class tended to marry each other.

But my uncle was in love with my aunt, and love prevailed. His mother didn't approve of their courtship and certainly not their marriage. They'd married before Robert was killed, while Uncle Oney was in still the army. Aunt Folia lived with his parents while he was stationed overseas. Uncle Oney's father loved my aunt dearly, while his mother would complain about the fact that they hadn't had any children yet. According to how my aunt told the story, living with them was difficult and uncomfortable. Her mother-in-law would say,

"You know, I would like some grandkids one day."

And my aunt would reply, "You know, it's hard for

animals to mate in captivity." (Of course, she would not say this out loud.) My aunt couldn't disrespect her mother-in-law. Grandma Lena would not have permitted it. Aunt Folia would visit Grandma sometimes and she would cry about how she was mistreated. Grandma Lena would say,

"Folia, whatever you do, don't disrespect Mrs. Harris."

Aunt Folia would say, "But, Mama…"

"It doesn't matter, Folia. Don't you ever disrespect her," Grandma told her.

She never did disrespect her mother-in-law, and it's a good thing she didn't. After Uncle Oney left the army and he and Aunt Folia moved to Nashville, his parents ended up moving in with them. After his father died, my aunt took care of the elder Mrs. Harris. She was consistently kind and loving, and the time came when Mrs. Harris told my aunt she was sorry for how she'd behaved. When she passed away, Aunt Folia inherited all of her possessions: mink coats, jewelry and furniture. Everything.

* * *

Uncle Oney died in 2012, and Aunt Folia passed away four years later. All of the beautiful things they owned together, including the items my aunt inherited from her mother-in-law were passed on to Mom and eventually to me. Since they never had children, and I had cared for them both in their elder years, I was their closest heir. In fact, I was the only remaining child on Mom's side of the family. The only niece and the only daughter. When I share that with people, they usually are stunned. Out of four healthy sisters, all of whom lived to see old age, how could I be the only surviving child? Cousin Sandra's death in the early eighties had made it so. After she died I never considered what that meant, the weight of it, until I became much older. As I aged, so did my aunts, uncles and parents.

In 2005, several years before my uncle and aunt died, I was living in the metro Atlanta with my husband, Mark and our family. We were working and serving in a major ministry in the area. One day on the way to church, the Lord spoke to Mark and told him that we needed to move back to Nashville the following year. We were obedient to the Holy Spirit's leading and returned the next year. I knew that the reason we were to return was to begin our ministry, but I didn't realize the other reason was because my family needed me.

Aunt Pat, Aunt Folia and Uncle Oney, and Mom and Daddy all were getting up in age and I needed to be there to look after them. One day, during my quiet time with the Lord, He told me that someone was getting ready to leave. I knew that meant someone was going to pass away. In fact, the Father always would give me some sort of warning before a family member died. Though I didn't know it at the time, in this instance it was Aunt Pat. She had just had cataract surgery; it was rough on her, but she came through it fine. At the time she was living in her own home, but after the surgery it became clear that she couldn't remain there by herself. Aunt Pat ended up in the hospital and from there we arranged to have her live at a nursing facility.

Two months later, I received a call at work. I was working as a part-time scheduler at an eye surgeon's office, and I was exhausted because I'd worked a double shift. The call was from Mom. She said the nursing facility had called her and that they'd taken Aunt Pat to the hospital. She had been in and out of the hospital so much during that time, that I didn't think too much of it. My office building was near the hospital, so it was easy for me to go over there to check on her. Mark picked me up from work and we went.

We entered Aunt Pat's room and she was propped up in the bed. Mom and Daddy had been there for a while waiting in the emergency room, so I sent them home. I asked her what the matter was, and she said that she felt like she had to vomit but she couldn't. The doctors told me that they did a scan of her abdomen and found that there was an obstruction. They said that they planned keep her overnight to run more tests the next day, and that since it was late, we should probably go home and rest.

The next morning, I was exhausted and had the worst headache that I could remember ever having. Mom and Daddy were too tired to go back to the hospital. I pulled myself together so that I could go see about Aunt Pat. When

I arrived, she was sitting up in bed again and started talking before I could make it to her bedside.

"What am I gonna do with my house Patricia?"

I had been trying to talk to her for a while about that, but every time I brought it up, she didn't want to discuss it. Apparently now was the right time. I needed to know her wishes so that I could make sure that everything happened in an orderly way.

"Aunt Pat, it's the Saturday before Memorial Day. I don't know what we can do at this point."

I didn't realize that she had a knowing she would be leaving here. I wasn't thinking of that at all. In my mind, I was thinking that her house had been sitting vacant for the past few months, and sooner than later we needed to determine what we were going to do with it.

The next day Mom and Daddy visited her. I needed rest and wasn't going to go, but the hospital called me and said Aunt Pat was not doing well, and that I should come. Mom and Daddy had been at the hospital earlier that day. When Daddy and I spoke he said, "I looked at her when I came in and she looked right through me. I believe she's probably ready to go. Her kidneys are shutting down."

Over the next couple of days, Aunt Pat was talking and very lucid. On Tuesday I was at work and the Lord said, "Leave now." At that time, we only had one car, so I asked my dear friend, Barbara, if she could take me and she agreed. I had called Marketta and my parents to tell them not to worry about coming because I was there.

Barbara and I walked in to find Aunt Pat sitting in her bed, her green eyes vibrant—beautiful and clear. I never recalled seeing her look so lovely. She greeted me happily.

"Hey Patricia," she said. She looked at my friend. "Barbara, how are you doing? You've got twin girls, right?"

My friend and I both were surprised that she remembered. Aunt Pat had only met her once or twice before and it was unusual for her to remember details.

"Yes, ma'am," Barbara replied.

The nurse came in and told us that they were getting ready to take Aunt Pat for a test.

"What test do I have to have now?" she asked. The nurse told her that the doctor wants to look at what's going on inside her body. "Patricia are you going be here when I get back?" she asked.

"Yes, Auntie," I said.

"You know, I had a dream about you last night. I dreamed you were at my house and it started raining. And you said, 'I'm going to go in the living room Aunt Permatis, I'll be back.' But you didn't come back. You didn't come back in the bedroom."

"I didn't?" I said.

"No. Isn't that interesting?"

"It sure is," I said.

"But you're going to be here when I get back from this test?" she asked again.

"Yes, ma'am" I said.

With that, the orderly wheeled my aunt out of the room. Barbara and I went into the waiting room. It couldn't have been more than fifteen minutes that had passed, when we heard an announcement,

"Would the Jones family please report to the nurse's station?"

Aunt Pat's last name was Jones, but it didn't register with me. I just wasn't expecting it, so I didn't budge. We heard the announcement again.

"Would the Jones family..." I came to myself.

"Oh, they're talking about us," I said. We got up and headed for the nurse's station and saw my aunt's doctor walking toward us from the opposite end of the hall. Two nurses followed closely behind him. Just as we met in the middle of the hallway, the doctor said,

"Patricia?"

"Yes," I said.

"Your aunt was really sick."

"Yes, I know," I said.

"She was sicker than what we realized."

I said, "Okay, well, she got the test, right? What did you find out?"

"No, ma'am," he said. "No, she crashed on the table.

I'm so sorry. We did everything…"

Barbara gasped, "Oh my God."

I still wasn't getting it. I think I didn't want to believe it so my mind just couldn't make sense of what they were saying. I continued,

"You said she crashed on the table? But you performed the te…" I didn't finish the last word. Suddenly it was clear. I understood. She was gone. I collapsed into a heap on the floor and began to cry.

"No, she told me to wait. I told her I would be here waiting for her," my voice rising.

Barbara crouched down and wrapped her arms around me. The doctor calmly began to share what happened. He said Aunt Pat told him that she had to vomit. They turned her on her side to allow her to do that comfortably. As they were re-positioning her on the table she said,

"I feel better now." And she died, gone to Glory.

I demanded to see her. They took me into the room where she was. Aunt Pat looked beautiful. Her skin was glowing, and she appeared to be many years younger.

"You told me to wait on you," I said, weeping. "You asked me to wait and I promised. I stayed and you left."

That was what her dream was about; she was leaving this earthly realm and she probably knew it.

I realized that I needed to notify my family. Here it was only fifteen minutes after I had told my daughter and parents to not come; now I needed to make this dreaded call. It was surreal. I called Mom and Daddy first. Daddy answered the phone.

"D…Daddy…" I began. "You and Mom don't have to come."

"What's going on?" Mom was in the background asking what I was saying. After I hung up with them, I must have called Marketta and shared the news with her. I don't remember much else about those phone calls. Marketta never did get over the fact that she didn't get to see Aunt Pat before she passed.

A couple of days later we went to the funeral home to make arrangements; me, Mark, Mom and Daddy, Aunt Folia and Uncle Oney, who was on a walker. They sat there around the table, elderly and gray-haired, some with their own health challenges, trying to decide what to do. Aunt Pat had no children and her husband had died long before. After a few minutes, I told them that Mark and I would handle everything and sent them home.

That day, watching my parents, aunt and uncle trying to make decisions, I came to the realization of the true position that I was in. I was, indeed, the only remaining child and niece in my Mom's family; I was the only heir. That also meant that I was going to be responsible for seeing to it that the rest of my family was properly looked after. That was 2008. And for the next decade, almost every two years, I would bury another family member.

Reflection

When I was adopted into the Parker family, I not only gained a mother and father, but I also received the gift of aunts and an uncle who were like second parents to me. I enjoyed many years of being treasured as a daughter. But as time would have it, I grew into a woman with my own family. And as I became older, so did my adoptive family. Adoption began to take on new meaning. My family had selflessly embedded me in their hearts. They'd cared for me so attentively, and now I was having to do the same.

It is similar with the family of God. When we enter in as heirs, we cannot become selfish, only focused on receiving the benefits of having a heavenly Daddy who is all powerful, all knowing, all gracious and sovereign. We should reach out to others, both within God's family and outside of it. Through the Father's love and the power of the Holy Spirit, He will show us how to nurture and care for our brothers and sisters in Christ, and those who join His family. God's family is eternal. John 3:16 says, "For God so loved the world, that he gave his only begotten Son, that whosoever believeth in him should not perish, but have everlasting life."

We often think of adoption within the context of receiving. The adopted child receives so much. In the natural sense, they receive the love and security of a new family. In a spiritual sense, they receive unmerited favor and blessings from God. But adoption really creates a two-way relationship of love between everyone involved; naturally it is unto death and spiritually unto eternal life.

CHAPTER FOUR

Learning My Religion

I got saved when I was twelve. I'm not sure I understood all that really meant at the time. I just knew that I didn't want to go to hell. And in the Pentecostal Church getting saved wasn't enough. We were taught that after you were baptized with water, you had to be baptized in the Holy Spirit. To do that, you had to tarry. That means you were expected to pray and wait until God allows you to receive a second baptism, in the person of the Holy Ghost. That praying and waiting could take hours, days, weeks or months. According to the church, it didn't matter how long it took, you had to work hard to receive it.

Of course, I know better now. We are filled with the Holy Spirit the minute we accept Jesus as our Savior. And we are baptized in the Holy Spirit when we ask the Father and remain open to Him moving. The way that we can know we've been baptized in the Holy Ghost is when we speak in tongues. But back then our church, and many others in the region, was governed by a religious spirit. We had to follow tradition and rules.

After I walked down the aisle and stood at the altar to give my life to Jesus, my pastor baptized me and another young man. We were then led into a room, where we were given some instructions on what to do, and the tarrying began. While a few older saints stood around praying and keeping watch over us, I did what they told me to. Seated in a chair, I rocked back and forth. I was praying and crying, spitting and slobbering all over the place, pleading the name of Jesus. "Jesus, Jesus, Jesus, Jesus, Jesus…" The saints on watch urged us to keep saying the Lord's name.

"Faster, say it faster. Come on," they said.

"Jesus, Jesus, Jesus, Je, Jee, Jeee…" I pleaded with the Father to baptize me in the Holy Ghost.

We were closed up in that small, hot room for hours. After a while, the man who'd also gotten baptized that day was able to get up and leave. The elders said he could go because he "got it." That left only me, still tarrying. Even though there were other people still in the room I felt alone. And I wasn't sure exactly what to expect when the Holy Ghost came. I knew tongues would come, but I had no idea how that was going to happen. All I knew was I hadn't received them yet, so I thought that I had to be doing something wrong. Eventually Daddy came to the room, and I was released.

"She didn't get it, Brother Parker. She only had stammering lips," one of the women said. Stammering lips is a reference to Isaiah 28:11, "For with stammering lips and another tongue he will speak to this people."

Daddy and I left the church and headed home. The car ride was quiet. When we arrived, I found Mom in their bedroom and immediately confessed.

"Mama, I didn't get the Holy Ghost yet," I said, eyes lowered and head down. I was so disappointed, I wanted to cry. "I've been tarrying like they said, and I didn't get it." I wasn't sure how she would respond, but I hoped she would make it all right.

"Patricia," she said. "You're not supposed to tarry."

Not understanding what she meant, I said, "But Mama, they told me…"

"I don't care what they told you. They only said you need to tarry and wait for the Holy Ghost, because that's what they did," she said, sitting me down next to her on the bed. "But that's not the truth. You don't have to tarry for what's already here."

Mom was telling me that I didn't have to work to be baptized in the Holy Ghost or to receive my tongues. I needed only to be open to receive it from the Father, and it would come in time.

* * *

As I was growing up, my parents both became strong believers, but they were in different places spiritually. Daddy was strictly Pentecostal and believed in being faithful to the house where God sends you. He belonged to one church in Clarksville for many years, where he was responsible for opening up the building every Sunday morning. He turned on the heat in the winter and the air conditioning in the summer. Even after we moved to Nashville, we remained members of that church for several more years, making the fifty-mile drive at least once a week. That was well before the interstate was built, so it made Sundays extremely long.

In 1970, we joined Unity Pentecostal Church in Nashville. That's the church where I grew up. Daddy was on the elder board and served as the Sunday School superintendent. We attended there as a family for a while until Mom stopped coming regularly. I know that it hurt Daddy to not have both his wife and daughter at church with him, but Mom just couldn't do it. She knew too much of the truth.

Before my parents adopted me, when Daddy was still in the military, he and Mom lived in several different states across the country. It was while they were living in Washington D.C. that they were exposed to the Charismatic movement. Mom and Daddy both got saved during that time. Together, they visited churches where they witnessed creative miracles happen right in front of them.

Even after they moved to Tennessee, those experiences and the true gospel stayed with Mom. Daddy couldn't get used to that way of doing church and was drawn to the Pentecostals. I think it was because the church was very orderly and traditional; his preference for discipline and structure probably drew him. Besides, there were some aspects of Pentecostalism that seemed to overlap with the Charismatic church, so he may have felt it was the best place for our family. Initially, Mom went along with him, but I think in her heart she knew there was more. In spite of their differences, my parents did compromise. Many summers, our vacations would include driving across the country to attend crusades and tent meetings.

***

As it turned out, Mom was right. I didn't have to tarry to be baptized in the Holy Ghost. About a month after I got saved, our church was having Friday night prayer. Daddy was attending, and I decided to go with him so I could play with some of my friends. That night though, the pastor did things a little differently. He called everyone in the church to come up to the altar, kids included.

We were separated from each other, so I didn't have any of my friends around. I knelt down and the next thing I knew I was slain in the spirit, laid out on the floor, flat on my back.

For a while I couldn't move at all and then I dared not to. I think I knew that the Lord was doing something in me. When I opened my eyes, I looked up and saw Daddy standing over me dancing and shouting, "Thank you, Lord! Thank you, Lord!" I had received my prayer language and was speaking in tongues, with tears streaming down my face. Some of the older saints danced around me rejoicing with Daddy, while others were telling me I needed to stop and say, "Thank you, Jesus." I didn't pay attention to them though. I knew I had been baptized.

That night, on the way home, Daddy was so happy. He said, "Patricia, the Holy Ghost ain't for everybody. It's only for special people." I nodded in agreement, thinking that I must be one of the special ones. Later, I came to understand the truth; that the Holy Ghost is for whosoever is willing to receive Him.

Growing up at Unity there was a lot that I didn't understand about how we treated each other, and people outside of the church. At times there wasn't much kindness or meekness being shown. A couple of years after I got saved, a young lady and her boyfriend came to the church. She was pregnant and couldn't have been more than sixteen. The church was across the street from some projects where they lived.

My parents had sheltered me from a lot of things so I'm not even sure I realized the girl was having a baby. But I did notice that they always sat in the back when they came, and that no one would sit with them. So, one day I decided to leave the front of the church, where the youth usually sat, and go back to say hello. After that, the young couple started attending regularly and each Sunday I sat with them. I just wanted to sit and talk to them so that they would feel welcome. Apparently, Sister Patterson, one of the mothers of the church, had been watching. After service one Sunday, she pulled me aside and told me that I didn't need to sit with them.

"Why can't I sit here?" I asked.

"Well, it's because she's 'in that way,'" Sister Patterson whispered the last part. I had no idea what she was talking about.

"What "way" is that?" I asked.

She hesitated, not really knowing what to say. When she saw my daddy, she told him what she'd said to me. After he explained it to me, I got the picture and stopped sitting with them.

In her own way, I know Sister Patterson was trying to protect me. I was impressionable and becoming a teenager myself, and even though they weren't much older than me these young people were clearly more advanced. But still, I don't believe the church showed them the love that we should have. Even though I was young, I knew that wasn't right. Because the girl was pregnant and unmarried, people in the church looked down on her and her boyfriend. The young couple ended up leaving the church. Interestingly, I would find myself thinking back to that experience just a few years later.

Unity's building had been a hospital in the early 1940s and 1950s, so the setup was kind of odd for a church. The building had two floors and we never really used the upper levels, which were for storage. When I eventually had a chance to go up to the second and third floors with some other kids. There hadn't been any remodeling done at all. I could tell that there used to be beds in the rooms. Then when we looked in a few more of the rooms, I saw that there was still equipment in them. It was creepy. Eerie sounds traveled down the halls and seemed to slip from room to room. I rarely went upstairs after that.

The main floor of the church was set up in a strange way, too. The front doors faced the street, but we entered the church through the back doors, from the parking lot. Since we had to enter through the back, it took longer to get to the sanctuary. Once you entered, the pulpit and choir stand were to the far right. The pews went straight back from the pulpit back to the left. But to access the pews, you had to walk all the way around.

We had about fifteen members back then. The church was founded by a woman, Pastor Minnie, who had been friends with my Grandma Lena. Pastor Minnie's sister, Sister Baker, was also a family friend, and when my grandmother died she became like another grandmother to me.

Our church environment and members were loving. I believe everyone meant well and truly loved God. But everything that we did or were instructed to do was motivated by control. Keeping a tight grip on the members was a mark of a religious spirit rooted in our church.

For example, women were not allowed to wear pants, makeup or fancy hairstyles, and were controlled by their husbands. Wives were to be seen and not heard, and to justify how women were treated, the men in the church often would misuse the scripture that wives are to submit to their husbands. In fact, 1 Corinthians 14:34-35 was, and still is, often used to prevent women from speaking in the church: "Let your women keep silence in the churches: for it is not permitted unto them to speak; but they are commanded to be under obedience as also saith the law. And if they will learn any thing, let them ask their husbands at home: for it is a shame for women to speak in the church."

In addition to being kept silent, women were not permitted to go to the movies or concerts. Nor could they listen to secular music. Mind you, this was during the 1960s, the era of Motown and fabulous black music, but I had no exposure to it at all. We were even forbidden to attend meetings hosted by ministers such as Kenneth Copeland or Fred Price when they came to town, largely because of the controlling and manipulating spirits that hung over our church. Our leaders feared that the people would follow the truth instead of tradition.

One Sunday, Sister Patterson, who had scolded me for sitting with the teen couple, rebuked me again. She was tall and very busty, and during service, she would shout with one arm holding up her bosom, and the other thrown back.

"Whoomp! Whoo!" she would holler over and over.

I would hold my hand over my mouth to hide the giggles. Brother Patterson, her husband, was much shorter and shaped like an egg. The couple had several children. One of their sons, Wendell, was known to stay in trouble. Sister Patterson would call out to him, "Wen-dayell! Wen-dayell get over here and sit down!" in her thick, twangy accent.

The day Sister Patterson approached me for the second time, was because she disapproved of a sleeveless dress I was wearing. It was mint green with a pleated skirt and had what looked like tiny cotton balls all over the bodice. It was very feminine and the prettiest dress that mom had bought me. I loved it. Plus, it was summertime, so it helped me to stay cool.

"Patricia, your arms don't need to be out like that. You need to tell your mama she needs to cover 'em up," she said.

I imagine it was convenient for her to correct me because, by then, Mom had stopped accompanying me and Daddy to Unity. Maybe she thought she was being helpful, but I knew she was just being nosy. And I knew I had to report to Mom what she had said. When we got home, I walked into the kitchen and sat down. I folded my hands and gently placed them in my lap. Mama was finishing up dinner. Sensing I had something to say, she looked over at me.

"Mama, Sister Patterson said to tell you that my arms need to be covered up," I said. Mom went from zero to sixty in a split second.

"Les-lie," she called after Daddy. "You not gonna have my daughter going over there to that church, and they talking about what she's goin' to wear. She is twelve years old..." She went on for a few minutes.

I don't remember all of what she said, but she was not happy. And I was glad because I didn't even know what Sister Patterson was talking about. After all, what was the matter with wearing a sleeveless dress when it's hot outside? It's like what minister Jesse Duplantis used to say to show how ridiculous the religious spirit can be, "If showing armpits is an issue then y'all got bigger problems. 'Cause I ain't seen an armpit yet that turned me on..."

* * *

As a teen the chatty, outgoing nature that I had as a little girl started to fade. I was no longer the child who would hold conversations with perfect strangers during bus rides with Aunt Folia. I didn't step out to introduce myself to people whom I was just meeting for the first time. I became painfully quiet. I would speak only when I was spoken to. And if I had an opinion about anything, I'd just keep it to myself. When I did say something, people would tell me to a "speak up" because they couldn't hear me. It was suffocating. I did have a lot to say. And a lot of the time I just wanted to be able to greet people and simply say hello. But the words wouldn't come out. Instead, I drew back into the shadows, not wanting to have attention focused on me, not having the courage to be seen or heard.

This shyness was reflected during a performance at a Christmas program at Unity that year. I was first soprano in the choir, and I was asked to sing "The First Noel" as a solo. I agreed to do it, but I was very nervous. My shyness was in full effect. Mom, Daddy, Aunt Folia and Uncle Oney all attended. Before I sang, Daddy pulled me aside and to coach me.

"Look in the audience, Patricia," he said. "If you don't see anyone smiling at you, just look at the clock."

And that's exactly what I did. I got up and sang the carol, but I didn't look into anyone's faces. Instead, I locked my eyes on the clock and didn't move them. At the very end, one of the other girls whom I'd invited to come on stage with me so that I wouldn't feel like I was by myself, finished the chorus with me. Daddy didn't like that, and on the way home from the performance he chastised me.

"You should have sung the whole song yourself, Patricia," he said. "You sing beautifully on your own."

"But Daddy, she just harmonized with me," I replied.

"Why did she have to be up there?" he asked.

"I don't know, Daddy. I just asked her to," I said.

I didn't know at the time why I had her finish the song with me. But now I realize that it was partly because I was so incredibly shy. The other part of it, though, was the limitations that Pentecostalism had placed on me. There were so many things that we could not do, so many things that we were told were displeasing to the Father, that I took a lot of that to heart. I think that I felt it would be better to shrink back instead of fully being who I was.

My release from being bound up in religion took some time, but eventually it did come. And it was largely due to Mom's influence. While Daddy and I faithfully attended Unity every Sunday, Mom was getting fed by other ministries. She learned the truth about who we become when we are born again. She gained a full understanding of Mark 16:17-18: "And these signs shall follow them that believe; in my name shall they cast out devils; they shall speak with new tongues; they shall take up serpents; and if they drink any deadly thing, it shall not hurt them; they shall lay hands on the sick, and they shall recover."

These were the things that my Mom believed and witnessed when the Holy Ghost was allowed to flow freely and without restraint—without the spirit of religion. On Saturday nights, Grandma Lena, Mom, and I would watch the godfather of the charismatic movement, Oral Roberts, on television. His services were so different than what we were doing at Unity. Grandma Lena was in her eighties, and while she loved the Lord, it was near the end of her life that she truly got an understanding of the importance of the Holy Spirit flowing freely. And Mom was a big part of that. When we'd go away to the crusades, my grandmother wouldn't come with us, but Mom would always come back and tell her about what took place. Eventually, I became more drawn to televangelists like Rev. Roberts and A. A. Allen, whom we'd seen at that very first tent meeting when I was five, and I grasped an understanding for myself. That truly was when my deliverance began.

Reflection

I believe that the religious traditions and rules of many denominations, including Pentecostalism, have caused believers like myself to suppress who we truly are. When we receive Jesus as our Lord and Savior we are born—adopted—of the Spirit of God. 1 Peter 1:23 says, "Being born again, not of corruptible seed, but of incorruptible, by the word of God, which lives and abideth forever." With our adoption, this birth the scripture speaks of, comes benefits.

Father God does not wait until you are saved to deliver benefits to you. In Revelation 13:8 we read that the Lamb was slain before the foundation of the world. So, all the provision you will ever need was established even before you were born! There's no need to work for it, to tarry, to perform to make it happen. Your adoption as a son or daughter of God gives you divine access.

A dear friend who is now with the Lord said, "God does what He did!" God provided healing before sickness ever came. Before you knew that you needed to be restored, restoration was here! It was the same way with Adam in the Garden of Eden. Everything was prepared before the woman came on the scene. That was God's first example of showing how He treats His beloved, adopted children. Hebrews 4:3 says, "For we which have believed do enter into rest, as he said, as I have sworn in my wrath, if they shall enter into my rest: although the works were finished from the foundation of the world."

This is the problem with religion. It deceives. Jesus did a complete work, but religion tells you there's more for you to do. Jesus said in Mark 7:13, "Making the word of God of none effect through your tradition, which ye have delivered: and many such like things do ye." We don't need tradition or rules. Under the new covenant of grace, all we will ever need has been completed through Jesus Christ.

MAY • 63

Mom, Aunt Folia and me, age 3 (1963)

Grandpa Repps and Grandma Lena (1959)

JAN • 69

Me at Christmas, age 9 (1969)

Aunt Folia and Uncle Oney
on their Wedding Day (1946)

CHAPTER FIVE

The Company You Keep

During the first couple of years in high school, I had very few friends. Two of the girls at Unity went to school with me, and they played basketball. One of their mothers and Mom would attend Kenneth Copeland's meetings when he came to town. While I didn't consider the girls to be close friends, they looked out for me, kind of like big sisters. They were seniors when I was in the tenth grade and used to hang out a lot at the movies or the bowling alley, but I was never invited. I once asked them why and one of them told me flatly:

"Pat, you know Elder Parker won't let you go. So, we don't bother to ask."

I couldn't argue with her. Daddy was very protective, and he rarely gave me permission to do anything social with them, or anyone really, inside or outside of church. He also couldn't stand for people to call me Pat. Along with my shy and quiet nature that had begun to develop, I didn't push back, even when it came to what people called me. I hated for people to call me Pat and Daddy would say to me repeatedly, "Your name is Patricia and that's what people should call you." I'd nod in agreement but never corrected anyone.

At school, I was friendly with most people, but not many boys until my sophomore year. That's when I got to know Eddie Jackson. I first was introduced to him through his cousin. In Daddy's job at the Veteran's Hospital he would often visit patients' homes, where he'd teach them and their caregivers how to perform dialysis treatments. Occasionally, I would go with him during follow up visits. Val, the daughter of one of his patients, and I hit it off and quickly became friends. It turned out that Eddie was her cousin. She would talk about him all of the time—constantly saying what a nice guy he was—but I didn't realize right away that I already knew him from school.

Eddie was very popular, and one day he just started talking to me in the hallway. After that, I noticed that every day between classes he would make it a point to walk over to my locker, to say hello or chat. Tall, slim, and funny, Eddie was very smart. We started hanging out regularly as friends. He was fun to spend time with and was very much a gentleman. He was also was "old school," which made him a little offbeat but still, everyone loved him.

Eventually, we became close and we would ride around town in his little MG convertible. Eddie's father was on the police force and well-known in Nashville. His parents had him when they were young, and his dad did the honorable thing by marrying his mom. It was obvious they loved each other. Surprisingly, my parents didn't have a problem with Eddie at all, and in fact, they really liked him. They'd met his parents a few times and respected his father highly.

In my teen years, I was tall and skinny. I didn't wear makeup and wasn't attractive like the beauty queens Eddie normally would hang around. Still, he would always seek me out. He'd be talking with his friends and if he saw me walking down the hall, he'd yell out, "Here comes my skinny baby!" I would reply playfully, "I am not your baby!" acting as though I didn't like him, even though I really did. While I just saw him as a friend, he was special to me.

One time I overheard one of his friends say, "Big Ed, you hang with her?" to which he replied, "Yeah!" as if he dared his friend to say anything else about it. He couldn't care less about how us spending time together looked to other people. He always told me that there was more to me than what those other girls had.

I knew Eddie was sweet on me. After a few months, he gave me a beautiful friendship ring with two hearts and a diamond in the middle. Though I think he wanted our friendship to develop into a girlfriend, boyfriend relationship it never did. I was so insecure at that time. Still extremely shy, I didn't speak up for myself and was self-conscious about my looks. I couldn't imagine how such a handsome, popular guy would want to be with me, so we stayed friends.

* * *

During my junior year, everything changed. That was the year I met Cynthia Franklin, the girl who I thought would become one of my life-long friends. We'd seen each other a few times on the bus ride to school and then during our lunch period. One day, we struck up a conversation, which started our friendship. We didn't have a lot in common, but she was easy to talk to and we got along.

Cynthia lived within walking distance from me, across the railroad tracks. I lived in my parents' six-bedroom house, and she lived in a much smaller house with her mother, father and four-year-old stepsister. Later, I learned that her parents were not married but were common-law husband and wife. Walking through the front door of Cynthia's small, frame home, you could see the living room, kitchen, bedrooms and straight through to the back door all at once—what's called a "shotgun" house in the South. Cynthia's family had moved from Michigan to Nashville, so she was still new to the area when we met.

As time went on, Cynthia and I began to spend more and more time together. My big sisters from church had warned me about becoming friends with her, but I didn't listen. When I brought Cynthia home to introduce her to Mom, it didn't go well. I had told her beforehand that I wanted her to meet my parents, so we went to my house after school. We stood at the back of my house, talking and laughing, when Mom suddenly appeared at the screen door.

"Mom, this is…" I could barely get Cynthia's name out before Mom's bright green eyes met mine, her lips pressed together. It was like she was staring right into me. She didn't have to say anything, I knew immediately that she didn't approve of Cynthia. After the introduction Cynthia and I walked to her house. I thought it would be better to go to hers than to make her feel uncomfortable at mine. Later that afternoon, when I came home Mom stopped me as soon as I set foot in the kitchen.

"Patricia, that girl is not for you." Of course, at seventeen years of age I respected my mother, but I thought she was being too harsh.

"How can you tell, Mom? I barely got her name out and…"

"She was hiding behind you, Patricia," she replied. "When y'all were standing on the stairs as soon as I opened the door, she shrunk back behind you. You can tell a lot from someone who doesn't look you in the eye." Mom paused and then repeated the first thing she said, "I'm going to tell you right now, that girl is not for you."

Despite Mom's disapproval, I remained friends with Cynthia. Mom went along with it, but I knew she didn't like it. Cynthia was fun, outgoing, and accepting. I didn't feel like I had to act a certain way with her. I could be who I was. At the same time, she could be who she was, too. I wore nicer clothes and I would let her wear some of my outfits. She was shapelier than me, but I would let her wear them anyway. When she returned my clothes some of them were stretched out and no longer fit, so I let her keep them.

Cynthia had a half-sister, Tina, who was a little older than us. She was Cynthia's father's child from another relationship, and she still lived in Michigan. One summer Tina came to Nashville to visit Cynthia's family, so I ended up spending some time with her. In Michigan, Tina lived what might be called "the street life." Looking at her, I could tell that she was into some heavy things, but at the same time there was a softness to her. She was very attractive, shapely like her sister, and had the most beautiful smile. Tina was also really nice to me.

One day when I was visiting them, Tina said, "Y'all wanna go out back for a little while?" Her eyes met Cynthia's as if they had an understanding.

"Okay," I said, and the three of us went into the backyard. We sat on the hood of an old car and talked. After a while Tina pulled a lighter and a weird-looking cigarette out of her pocket. Even though I had been sheltered, I knew what it was.

They lit up, and that sharp, skunky smell surrounded us. I wasn't about to join in with them, but I wasn't going to leave either, so I just sat there looking at the birds or whatever else I could to take my attention off of what they were doing. Tina didn't pressure me to smoke, but she made sure I participated. She took a long drag from the joint and slowly blew smoke in my face. They both fell out laughing as I coughed and gasped for air. I know they looked at me like I was fresh off of the market. I had no experience with some of the things they were into. In a lot of ways, they were much more advanced than I was. But they didn't push me. I never did learn how to roll up a joint and we didn't drink or anything like that. When I had enough of the smoking though, I told them to stop and they did.

About three months later, Cynthia called me. Mom answered the phone and handed me the receiver. Cynthia said, "Tina's gone." She'd overdosed, and her little boy was the one who found her. He tried to wake her up but couldn't. Cynthia's family wasn't sure if it'd happened accidentally or if her boyfriend was somehow involved. The street life had grabbed hold of Tina and swallowed her up. She and Cynthia's father was distraught and wanted to go up to see his daughter one last time, but she'd been cremated before he'd gotten a chance to. Cynthia told me later that Tina had said that when she died to sprinkle her ashes in the ocean so she could travel all over the world. I think she knew that she would die young. That was just the life she lived.

By the end of that year, Mom's sensitivity to the Holy Spirit had begun to manifest strongly. Cynthia's influence was catching up with me and I was starting to move too fast. She had been telling me about her boyfriend, and how nice he was. He was in a singing group and she said there was a guy, Richard, who sang with him that I should meet. She suggested I ask Mom if I could spend the night with her. The guys could pick us up from her house. That way, I could meet Richard and we'd go out and have a good time.

So, I did just what we discussed. I asked Mom if I could spend the night at Cynthia's, but I told her we were going to hang out with some other girls from school. Slowly, Mom responded "yes," in a way that was drawn out as if she was thinking about her answer at the same time that she was giving it. I think that even though she believed Cynthia was not the kind of friend I needed, she also realized that I didn't have many friends and I needed to be social and have fun.

The day came and after school, instead of riding the bus home I got off with Cynthia at her stop. When we got to her house, we closed ourselves up in her bedroom and planned out our night. I was eagerly anticipating the evening and time seemed to be dragging. Suddenly, a thought popped into my head. What if Mom changed her mind and I wouldn't be able to go? Sure enough, a few minutes later I happened to glance out of the window and saw Mom pulling into the driveway. I immediately knew what that meant. She must've told Daddy that I was planning to go out with some friends and spend the night at Cynthia's, and he'd said no. I just knew that's what it was. I definitely hadn't told my parents about the young man, Richard, that I was meeting. And I hadn't really thought the plan through in case something went wrong. When you have parents who hear from the Holy Ghost, getting over on them is not that easy.

Cynthia's mom called to us, "Patricia, it's your mother."

I told Ms. Franklin that I knew she'd come. I asked her to not let Mom know I was there, and instead to tell her we'd left. Ms. Franklin stared at me blankly, my eyes pleading with hers. Cynthia and I stayed holed up in her room, but I cracked the door slightly so I could peek out. Ms. Franklin opened the front door and greeted Mom.

"Good evenin' Ms. Franklin, I'm looking for Patricia. Is she here?" I could hear mom inquiring.

"No, Mrs. Parker, she and Cynthia left out a little while ago," Ms. Franklin said. I could see Mom's head drop slightly and her shoulders lift as she took a deep breath. Ms. Franklin added, "They won't be back 'til late, so is she still staying the night?"

"I know I said she could, but her father wants her to come on home," Mom replied. Her eyes quickly scanned Ms. Franklin's living room and kitchen as if she was looking for any sign of me. "But if they've already left...are you sure they're gone?" Mom asked. She clearly had a sense that something wasn't right.

"Yes Mrs. Parker, I'm sure," said Ms. Franklin.

I heard their muffled goodbyes and the door closed. Cynthia and I sighed with relief. I quickly moved over to the window, and watched Mom slowly walk to her car. I could tell that she was concerned about me and what I was really up to. But she also was worried about having to tell Daddy that I was gone. I couldn't imagine what his reaction would be. I turned from the window and Ms. Franklin was standing in the bedroom doorway. As many times as I'd been in her home, she'd never looked at me the way she did then.

"Patricia, don't you ever ask me to lie to your mother again," she said firmly. "Ever."

Me and Cynthia's mothers may have been from different sides of the tracks, but they respected each other. I nodded and told her I was sorry. A little while later, Cynthia's boyfriend and Richard picked us up for the double date. They were part of a singing group—a quartet—that sounded just like The Spinners and we were headed to hear them audition. Prior to this, other than my friend Eddie, I'd had very little exposure to boys. Even when I would try to innocently spend time with a boy one-on-one it seemed like Daddy would show up out of nowhere. The only boys I really had spent time around was family; we'd get together with my cousins, Daddy's brothers' kids, during the summer. Still I had managed to at least have my first peck—I wouldn't even call it a kiss—with one of the boys who lived nearby.

After the audition we all went and got something to eat and then ended up at the house of someone the guys knew. It wasn't a party, but the house was full of people—more people than I'd ever been around at one time. There were things happening I wasn't used to seeing and being around. It was intense, and I felt like my head was spinning. It was like being in a movie. Richard and I ended up in a room, alone. In a split second, I made a life-changing decision. I definitely enjoyed Richard's company, and by the time we left that night I knew that I wasn't the same.

Very early the next morning there was loud knocking at the Franklins' front door. It was Mom. I packed up my things so we could go home. It was hard for me because I knew that the night before I had been somewhere I shouldn't have been, doing things I had no business doing. I knew that I had lied. And I could see the worry on her face.

After that night, Richard and I began seeing each other and talking regularly on the phone. Our relationship was budding. I introduced him to my parents, and they were respectful, but quiet. Their silence told me exactly how they felt, and I knew it was the same way Mom felt about Cynthia.

Richard lived on the other side of the tracks, too. His house was actually right next to the railroad tracks. I liked him very much. He was a hard worker, lived a clean life, dressed very well and had a wonderful sense of humor. We laughed so much. He even came to church with us on occasion. I knew that Richard wanted more out of life than where he was right then, and I admired that about him. As we got closer, our attraction to each other grew stronger and, naturally, we responded to the attraction.

A few months later, I found out that I was pregnant. I was very surprised, though I'm not sure why. I knew how babies were made. And I knew that when you play with fire, you get burned. But obviously I was not thinking at all about the possibility of having a baby.

I hadn't been feeling well so Mom took me to the doctor. The doctor examined me, and we found out I was expecting. Mom was devastated. Yet, it was almost like she already had a knowing. It's like she had already traced back to the months before when I'd lied about what we were doing at Cynthia's house; when Ms. Franklin lied about my not being there. I knew that she knew that was the night it all started.

The doctor's visit with Mom was bad enough, but next I had to tell Daddy. That terrified me, so Mom ended up telling him for me. The hardest part was the idea of the church members having to know. Fornication was clearly a sin and frowned upon and even worse than that, Daddy was a church leader and I didn't want to embarrass him.

When Mom finally told Daddy, he was so hurt. I could see the disappointment in his eyes. Appearances were important to him and I knew he was worried about how things would look to people—especially in the church.

Daddy didn't look at or speak to me for a while. He couldn't. I think it was hard for him to grasp that his little girl, for whom he'd sacrificed so much and taken so much care in protecting, was now a pregnant, unmarried teenager. I begged my parents to keep the pregnancy between us. They honored my request and decided not to tell my aunts and uncles until after the baby was born.

After they got over the initial shock, my parents slowly adjusted to the reality that they would be grandparents. They were forced to. I was so thin, that it was very easy to see that I was expecting. For me, I was ashamed about the pregnancy mostly out of fear of what the church members would say. It turns out that was justified because I later found out that the pastor had told Daddy that he should put me out of the house because of it. I thank God that Daddy thought better of that and never even considered it. But aside from the shame I initially felt, looking back I can see how God's hand of favor rested upon me during that time in my life.

My parents owned a laundromat, and Mom and I would sometimes go to collect the change, clean up and ensure that the machines were working properly. There was a white lady named Jewel who often did her laundry there. She was a heavy smoker, so her voice was deep and raspy. We were very friendly with each other.

One day, Jewel invited us to her apartment, which at that time was located in the projects across the street from the laundromat. As it turned out, Jewel was a gifted seamstress. She told me that she wanted to gift me with a maternity dress. She had to convince me as I wasn't sure about looking too nice as a pregnant girl. Mom wasn't comfortable with it either. But eventually I picked out a pattern. The next day I went to the fabric store and purchased a stunning emerald green, crepe material and delivered it to Jewel. Within a couple of weeks, she called Mom to let her know the dress was ready.

The first time I saw the dress, it took my breath away. It had a large cowl neck and moved effortlessly when I walked. When I sat down it draped across the floor. It was the most elegant piece of clothing that I'd ever owned. Mom protested that I didn't need to be wearing anything so fancy, that I didn't need to draw attention to myself in my condition, but I loved it so much and was determined to keep it. And Jewel said I had a right to. She said that I ought to be beautiful. So many of the young girls who were expecting wore t-shirts, with their pants unbuttoned and bellies hanging out. She said I was not that kind of girl. She really stood up for me and her words encouraged me so much that Mom let it be.

I already loved to dress well and receiving my gorgeous, green gift lifted me. I decided that through the rest of my pregnancy I would make an effort to look good. As the months went on, I would show up fully—very pregnant and always sharp. At that time I'd begun attending New Life, a predominantly white Pentecostal church, with Mom. When I wore that dress with my stilettos on, I held my head high. No one could deny that I was one beautiful, pregnant seventeen-year-old.

Around the same time, I decided to attend a school created specifically for pregnant teenagers. It was small, as there were no more than twenty girls there at the time. Some, like me, were there for their first time and others already had at least one child. The school had excellent programs, good, nutritious food and the building was nicely appointed. I enjoyed my time there.

Almost right away, the principal and staff pulled me aside and asked if I would mentor some of the other girls. I also was given a job to work at the front desk, answering phones and doing whatever the principal needed to be done. While there, I met a woman who wanted to do a documentary about me, covering my pregnancy and the plans I had for the future. Initially, I was ashamed of being an unwed mother. But over time that shame began to fade because of the Father's grace toward me. He made sure that I knew I was yet special. He had plans for my life and other people could see it.

Reflection

There is nothing you can do to stop Father God from loving you. He loves His children so much and desires the very best for us. Even when we do wrong, sometimes out of ignorance and other times knowingly, He yet remains near. His plans for us never change. Once we are adopted into His family, that's it. We're in. We are entitled to his inheritance and there is nothing that we can do about it.

God had a path that was clearly marked out for me. He arranged for Leslie and Dahlia Parker to take me into their home and raise me. I'm sure that they were not fully aware of the plans He had for my life. But they didn't need to—the Holy Spirit knew. Hebrews 4:13 says, "Neither is there any creature that is not manifest in his sight: but all things are naked and opened unto the eyes of him with whom we have to do."

And because my parents were born-again believers they operated in the Spirit of discernment. They were raising me to follow after godliness and holiness, which was leading me to follow Father God's plans for me. But instead of being obedient, I thought I knew better. I thought I was grown. Isn't that what we do with our parents as teenagers? Isn't that the attitude we sometimes take with the Lord? We tell Him that we know better, as if He hasn't seen what lies ahead.

Part of our inheritance through spiritual adoption is the gift of the Holy Spirit. Through my mother, the Holy Spirit was trying to give me a warning. Hebrews 3:15 says, "While it is said, today if ye will hear his voice, harden not your hearts, as in the provocation." Yet even though my heart was hardened to His voice to an extent, that didn't cancel His plans for me. He still showed me favor and love, and re-routed me back to the path He carved out for me.

CHAPTER SIX

Father's Provision

When I found out I was pregnant, I had a mixture of emotions. I was excited. I'm not sure why, but I was happy to be having a baby. I also felt terrible because I knew that my parents were deeply disappointed. This was not what they wanted for me. The pain that my parents showed at first made it really hard for me to interact with them. As the months passed, they wavered back and forth between expressing support and anger. But the main message I remember from that time was Mom saying to me that I was not the first one, and I wouldn't be the last. That meant a lot. Because, especially within the Pentecostal Church, I felt as if I were the only young lady to have committed this great sin. But that simply wasn't true. Even though she was struggling with it, Mom knew that I was struggling, too. And she encouraged me the best way she knew how.

My parents didn't intentionally make me feel ashamed, but I knew that I had let them down. I knew that every time they saw my growing belly, they would be reminded of what I'd done. So out of respect for them I spent most of my pregnancy at home in my bedroom. When I came home from school, I went straight to my room. Instead of eating dinner as a family like we'd always done, I would wait until Mom and Daddy finished and had cleared the kitchen, before going in to get my food. I ate in my room to avoid any chance of being in the kitchen with them at the same time. I now know that there was a spirit of isolation that kept me in my room, ashamed. The enemy has a way of striking hard when you are down, and he did his best to keep me in a low place. The amazing thing is that at the same time this was happening, God was lifting me up.

I began to hear from the Father very clearly. The most common way He communicated with me was through vivid dreams. One night in particular, I woke up screaming. Mom and Daddy came running into the room, thinking something was happening with the baby. I shared that I'd had a terrible dream and told them what it was about. I saw Richard's family there and they seemed to be calling me to them. Richard wasn't present. It was as if his family was saying it was okay for me to come with them, as if they were welcoming me. Then I saw snakes. I interpreted the dream to be a warning that let me know I was not to marry Richard. We had been talking about marriage and I'd been asking God what I should do? Getting married would have been the honorable thing to do; he was a good young man and we loved each other. But the dream confirmed that God was clearly telling me no. During that time, I also dreamt a lot about the return of the Lord Jesus Christ. And even though I couldn't explain how, I knew that the Lord told me I would have a boy and to name him Joshua David. I kept most of these things to myself because I felt that people wouldn't believe me.

I was experiencing some powerful things in the Lord for the very first time. Throughout my pregnancy I cried out to the Father, ready to receive more of Him, more of His love for me. And He answered in amazing ways. A couple of sisters from Unity who were a little older than I was visited the house a few times. They didn't seem to care at all that I was pregnant, and their dad was a lead deacon like mine. That really encouraged me.

I continued attending New Life. Mom would come with me at times, but even on the Sunday or Wednesday nights that she didn't attend, I was there. I was the only black member, so culturally, the environment was very different for me. But I never felt alone or uncomfortable because the pastor and members didn't treat me like a token. In fact, it was just the opposite. Everyone embraced me with the love of Christ, even though I was a very pregnant, unwed teenager. Every time I went, they welcomed me and my unborn baby and did not attach any type of stigma to either of us.

If I didn't have a ride, I would take the Nashville Metro bus to church. Maintaining my commitment to stay sharp, I'd be dressed to the nines, standing at the bus stop in the prettiest dresses, full make up and my signature stilettos. I'd always arrive early, go straight to the altar and just lie there praying, big belly and all. Those were some of the most intimate times I had with the Lord. No one else would be there, I could just cry out to Him and rest in His presence. I believe that was a period of strong impartation from the Father; it was one of the most precious times in my life.

A group of middle-aged ladies at the church literally adopted me. They greeted me warmly every time they saw me, and we would often talk about the goodness of God and just everyday life. A couple of months before I was set to deliver, they threw me a lavish baby shower. It was held at the church and everything from the decorations to the food was coordinated in excellence. I reminded them, as I often did, "But y'all know I'm not married." They responded that they knew, but it didn't matter. I came home with so many gifts for the baby, Mom and Daddy were shocked at how I'd been blessed.

Around that time, Daddy's brother Addison and his wife, Minnielee, came down from Connecticut to visit. Mom had prepared a huge meal for them to have when they arrived in town that evening, and I baked my first homemade chocolate cheesecake. Being as pregnant as I was, I was very hungry and decided to join the family and eat at the table. I was sitting next to Aunt Minnielee and for a while everyone ate, laughed and shared stories. I remained mostly quiet, trying not to draw attention to myself. Finally, I leaned over and said softly, "Aunt Minnielee, I'm going to have a baby."

"Well hell, girl, I didn't think it was a basketball sittin' up in there," she replied loudly. Surprised at how straightforward she was, I said, "I just wanted you to know."

"Honey, you're alright," Aunt Minnielee said, patting my hand.

Then, Uncle Addison chimed in. "You're alright girl, go on, you're alright."

It was settled. Right there at the dinner table in front of my parents, my aunt and uncle validated me. They didn't care that I was eighteen, pregnant and unmarried. In their eyes, it was no big thing. So, I sat at the table and ate well.

I experienced God's abundance and favor until the very end of my pregnancy. Every now and then, toward the end of my pregnancy, Daddy, Mom and me would go out to dinner as a family. One evening we went to an authentic Italian restaurant. I sat there, again trying to conceal myself out of respect for my parents. The waitress came over to our table to greet us. She took one look at me and exclaimed loudly, "Oh my goodness, you're gonna have a baby!" I could've melted into the floor right there. And I'm sure Mom and Daddy didn't appreciate the attention either. I shrunk down in my chair.

"I've got all these maternity clothes I would love to give you," the server said, smiling.

"Okay…" I said shyly.

Mom and Daddy just smiled. I think they were beginning to see that I actually was going to be okay. Between Daddy's family's acceptance, and the blessings from people God divinely connected me to, it was clear that His hand was over me and my baby who was coming soon.

When Joshua decided to enter the world, I was home alone with Mom. Daddy's job had him traveling a lot during that time and he had just left for a business trip. Mom made a nice dinner for me: pork chops, turnip greens and macaroni and cheese. I ate like my life depended on it. About forty-five minutes later we were in the den watching a movie and all of the sudden, sharp pains hit my belly.

"Mom…"

"What?"

"I'm cramp-…" I couldn't even get the word out fully before Mom jumped up and off of the couch. She grabbed her pocketbook, keys and my packed suitcase.

"Come on, we're going now!"

Outside, Mom hopped into the driver's seat of her car and pulled off so quickly that I barely had a chance to close the passenger door. I held on tight. Mom didn't have a whole lot of experience being behind the wheel. She hadn't started driving until a few years earlier, and even then, she didn't go far and not very often. Before that Daddy drove her everywhere. So, there we were, me and my drag-racing mama on our way to Vanderbilt Hospital. From our house, we had to round a sharp curve before getting to the main street of the hospital. Mom hit that turn at high speed and we were leaning so far to the left, it felt like the tires were barely gripping the road. But she got us there in one piece.

A nurse met us at the entrance with a wheelchair and Mom walked in with me. I remember feeling nervous, trying to anticipate what was coming next. At 9 p.m. another nurse came from around her desk to admit me.

"Oh, you're having a baby," she smiled widely.

"Yes," I said, wincing as a labor pain pierced my side.

"Okay, I'll see you later," I turned to see Mom's back as she headed for the exit, leaving me there. We'd never talked about what would actually happen when I gave birth. She made sure I had my bag packed, but we never talked about her staying with me—or leaving either, for that matter. I'm not sure I thought about it before then, but I was surprised that she left.

By the time I was admitted and taken to my room, my dinner decided that it was not going to stay put. I was miserable; I was vomiting, and labor pains were coming more regularly. I'd cry out, it hurt so badly. Some of the nurses were rough with me. They looked at me as if they were thinking, "Well you laid down to have this baby, now suck it up!" All I could think about was one of my aunts telling me that I would probably die in childbirth anyway because I was so young.

My labor was progressing slowly, so a nurse came in with a long instrument to break my water. As soon as it broke, she left the room. I ended up lying in the amniotic fluid, with vomit all over my gown, bed and the floor. No one cleaned any of it up. The nurse came back to put in an IV, so that I stayed hydrated. She couldn't get the vein in my right hand, which was closest to the IV, to cooperate. So, she yanked my left arm over my body to reach and inserted the needle in that hand instead.

I had no idea what having a baby was supposed to be like, but this was horrific. I didn't know what in the world I was supposed to be doing now. I'd gone to the doctor for my monthly check-ups. I'd taken my prenatal vitamins. I'm sure we had some general discussions at the doctor's office about childbirth. But no one coached me or talked to me about what to expect during the birth. I'd never felt so alone in my life.

Finally, a couple of nurses came in and told me to start pushing. I pushed and someone said they saw his head.

"Oh, he's got a head full of hair!"

How do you know my baby is a 'he'? I thought. There were no ultrasounds back then so how could they possibly know? The Lord had revealed it to me, but how did they know?

The pain was so intense, I got scared and stopped pushing. My baby stopped crowning. All of a sudden, an African American nurse appeared at my bedside.

"You gon' have this baby!" she growled. She pushed down hard on my stomach with her forearm.

"I'm not gonna have this baby," I yelled. "You're hurting me!"

She left the room. I believe she thought that she was helping me. But after all I'd already been through what she did just made the experience more terrifying.

"Lord," I prayed silently. "I'm not gonna have this baby. I'm doing my best, but I don't know how to do this." Tears streamed down my face. I really thought that I was not going to be able to give birth.

From the time that I was admitted at 9 p.m. to 9 a.m. the next morning I was in severe pain and crying out with each contraction. I was trying to hold the screams in. The woman that I shared a room with also was in active labor. There was a partition between us, but it couldn't block out her screams. By then, my nerves were shot and then all I could do was moan through the pain. My roommate finally had her baby and I remember them saying it was six pounds.

After she was discharged my obstetrician, Dr. Warren, came to see me. He saw me hanging over the side of the bed, and the vomit on the floor. He walked over, gently touched my foot and said, "Miss Parker, you've had a rough night, haven't you?"

"Yes sir, I have," I replied. I started to cry.

"I'm gonna help you deliver this baby. We're going to go ahead and use forceps. Is that alright?"

"Yes, sir," I said, relieved to finally have someone show me some compassion.

A few minutes later, a couple of nurses returned and gave me some numbing medication. I was taken to a delivery room, and with the help of forceps Joshua David was born. The nurses weighed him and said he was eight pounds and thirteen ounces. I could not understand how a baby that big came out of such a tiny space, especially since I was so skinny. They wrapped him up and put him in the incubator. He was fair skinned with slick, black hair. The nurses rolled me back to my room and asked me what I wanted to eat. I was so hungry! I told them I wanted fried chicken. Soon after that, Mom stuck her head in the doorway.

"Did you have it yet, Patricia?" she asked.

"Yes, Mom. He's here," I responded, nodding to the bassinet in the corner.

She walked over and picked him up. He was so heavy for her petite frame that she had to prop her arm up while she held him. I watched her as she gazed at him.

"Thank you, Jesus," I whispered. Somehow, I knew that was what she needed.

When we came home from the hospital, I was a nervous wreck. Daddy was due back in town soon and I wasn't sure what he would say when he saw Joshua David. After his birth, Mom told me to sleep in the guest bedroom where I would have more room with the king-sized bed. Joshua was lying in the middle of the bed, and I was in the den when Daddy came home, a few days later. He spoke to Mom and then to me and headed down the hallway toward their bedroom, luggage in hand. I peeked out of the den to watch as he turned his head to look into the guest room and saw Joshua in the bed asleep. I observed him as he stood and looked at Joshua, and I breathed a sigh of relief.

Within a day or two the sweet newness of Joshua's arrival had worn off for Daddy. The baby was crying every two hours.

"Can you do something to stop him from crying?" he asked. I looked at Daddy blankly. This was all new to me. I didn't know what to do.

Eventually, I got the hang of things and my parents got accustomed to having a newborn in the house. But Daddy would not hold him, until one day he was forced to. While I was pregnant, I'd developed an abscess in one of my teeth. Now that I'd had the baby, I couldn't take the pain anymore. I was up all night and the next day Daddy decided to take me to the dentist. We had to take Joshua with us. After I checked in, I turned to Daddy and told him that he would need to hold the baby while I was having the procedure. He looked like he wanted to be anywhere but there at the moment. But he did it. The receptionist said, "Mr. Parker, don't you drop that baby now."

"I'm not gonna drop him, I'm not gonna drop him," he said.

I went back and had the tooth pulled. When I came out and saw Daddy holding my baby, it just felt so good. After we got home he still wouldn't hold him, and I couldn't understand why. I told Mom that he's gonna have to hold Joshua more. A few days later he was watching TV in the den.

I ran in and said, "Daddy, I need you to hold Joshua. I've got to do something." While Daddy protested, I placed Joshua in his arms. "No, I just need you to hold him for a minute," I said and left the room.

I went out into the hallway to join Mom and we peeked in the doorway. Daddy was just looking at Joshua, talking to him and asking him how he was doing. I thanked Jesus. From that point on, Daddy was more comfortable with his grandson and they began to build a strong bond.

My church family fell in love with Joshua. I remember the pastor lifting him up to the Lord to dedicate him. The Lord spoke a word over him; Mom was with me that day. After that, Joshua was always at church with me on Sundays and

Wednesday nights. Mom and Daddy took to my son as if he were their own. In fact, one day Aunt Folia told me that Mom thought Joshua was her and Daddy's child. I'm sure having my baby there reminded her of the baby boy they'd lost many years earlier. Mom and Daddy helped me raise Joshua. Mom took care of him while I went to school and worked, and when he was old enough to go to daycare, she would drop him off and pick him up.

As Joshua grew, I began to call him by his middle name, David. He loved to spend time with my father. When we'd attend Unity, he'd want to sit right next to Daddy in the deacon's pew. Visitors often thought David was Daddy's son, they were so much alike.

I began to settle into my roles of being both a daughter and a mom. I eventually broke off my relationship with David's father and began to focus on my future. We parted on good terms and remained friends.

During my senior year of high school, I worked as a secretary for a recruiter in downtown Nashville. My parents wanted me to go to college after graduation, but they were not familiar with process. I think that maybe they expected more assistance and direction from the school to prepare me. I didn't feel as if I was college material, so I didn't pursue it. I was perfectly happy pursuing a career and raising my son in my parents' home. But the next step in my life was significant and beyond what I could imagine.

Reflection

Becoming an unwed teenaged mother could have turned out very differently for me, had I not been adopted by the right parents. Through their disappointment at my situation they were determined to stand by me and keep me encouraged. It was the same for Father God. Despite the fact that I acted out in disobedience, He never left my side.

I, on the other hand, ran from God because of my mistakes. I thought, *God I'm just going to just walk away when I mess up, because I'm sure You may not love me anymore.* But, the Lord told me that He needed me to stay at His feet. It's true that He repels sin. Jesus, His only Son, gave His life for sin. And the Lord even turned away from His only begotten Son on the cross because of that sin he bore. But because of our adoption as the Father's Sons and Daughters, we are entitled to remain in His presence, even in the midst of our disobedience.

The Lord showed me a vision: *You were there, Daughter, and I was here,* He said. *There was a wide gap between the two of us. Now tell me,* He asked, *who do you think was sitting in the gap?* He explained that the enemy was in the gap. As a result, I was hearing more of the enemy's voice than the Father's. The Lord began to say how much He cared for me and wanted to nurture me through my mistakes. 1 John

1:9 says, "If you confess your sin God is faithful and just to forgive you and cleanse you from all unrighteousness." If we honestly ask the Father to forgive us in Jesus' name and ask the Holy Spirit to help us, He promises to do what we ask.

Clockwise from left: Mom, Aunt Tina, Aunt
Folia and Aunt Pat (1991)

Daddy at work (1980)

CHAPTER SEVEN

Sunday Suits and Overalls

Joshua was thriving and as he grew, I learned that he was naturally creative. When he started walking, he would toddle into the kitchen open the cabinets, and drag out pots and pans. I'd give him a spoon and he'd play those pots like drums. Most of the time either Mom or I would be in the kitchen while David was making his music. One day, Daddy came into the kitchen and saw David playing with the cooking pans and asked Mom, "Is David playing on the floor with the same pots and pans you cook out of Dahlia?" As he got older, we noticed that he could keep a beat. We realized David could play the drums, which he can still do now. He also was extraordinary at drawing freehand. He was so talented.

I continued attending New Life church with David, who was then about three years old, at my side. While the church was coming out of a religious mindset, I was still very much tied to my upbringing, which was rooted in religion. For me, this included showing up for service in my Sunday best: a nice dress or suit and heels.

Around this time, a traveling ministry had stopped over in Nashville for a few months and decided to return to New Life on a Wednesday night. They'd visited with our church during previous ministry trips and came back whenever they were in town. After service some of the church women told me that they had someone for me to meet. They had been telling me about him for a few weeks now, and finally they intended to introduce us. Apparently, the times his ministry had been there before, I had not. That night, though, I was sitting on the front row when they said, "Patricia, he's coming over here now."

I casually turned around to look and immediately whipped back around in my seat. I told them, "The devil is a liar!" I couldn't tell you exactly what he looked like, or how he seemed. All I could focus on was the fact that the man had on white painter's overalls. At church! He stood in front of me, and I looked him up and down thinking, "What kind of mess is this?" To his credit, the overalls were clean, but still... The ladies introduced us.

"Patricia, this is Mark Douglas."

I cut my eyes and said flatly, "Hello, nice to meet you."

Clearly offended by my reply, he barely spoke. Typically, after Wednesday service, several church members would gather for dinner at Shoney's, so shortly after the awkward introduction we all headed out to eat. At the restaurant, Mark sat across from me at the table. He was proper, placing a napkin neatly in his lap as if he had manners. Obviously, he didn't if he was wearing those overalls. Because he was sitting right in front of me, I went ahead and spoke up.

"So...you travel?" I asked.

"Yes," he responded dryly.

This was going to be an interesting night. Maybe I was thrown off by our introduction at the church, but I immediately regretted the next question that I asked him.

"Well, do you ever plan on getting married?" I honestly don't know why I asked that. I wasn't thinking about us getting married. I'd just met the man. I like to think that I was just asking in general.

"I'm not getting married," he responded, taking his napkin and wiping his mouth. Surprised at his answer, I asked another question.

"Oh, well is there a reason why you don't want to get married?" I asked.

Putting down his fork, he looked directly at me and said, "If the Lord wants me to get married, He'll have to come down here Himself and tell me I'm to get married."

Well why did he say that, Jesus? And more importantly, why did I even care? The next thing I knew, I went completely off on him.

"You know, you're not that special that the Lord's got to come down to tell you anything. Who do you think you..."

In an instant I realized I was out of order and acting totally outside of my nature. I stopped talking and Mark just sat there staring at me. It was quiet for a moment before he replied, "As I said."

Oh, I had to repent for the things I thought about him after that. Just thinking about those three little words, *as...I... said...*nearly set me off again. Who did he think he was? Sitting there in those tacky white overalls, acting all manneredly at the table. Besides, he talked very properly as if he'd gone to school for it or something.

After that night, we would see each other again at church since the ministry he was part of decided to remain in Nashville for a while. In a few weeks' time I began to really see Mark for who he was. The man was handsome—the tall, dark kind. And then one day he sang with the worship team, and he really had an anointed voice. Instead of those white overalls, which I never did see again, he would wear blue jeans, cowboy boots and dress shirts to church, and they fit him quite well. At that point I knew that I was beginning to take an interest in him.

We started to talk more during the Wednesday evening fellowships after church. Eventually I gave him my phone number and we started going out. By then, I'd had a really good chance to look at him up close and realized the man was very good looking. I would look at his eyes and he had long eyelashes. It almost looked like his eyes were outlined. I don't know if the Lord was highlighting his eyes to me or what, but they were beautiful. David was about four then and he was always with me at church. One of the first things Mark said to me was how he noticed the loving way that I interacted with my son. I really liked that he noticed, and that he acknowledged David.

One of our favorite places to go on dates was the Nashville Airport. At that time, you could drive right up to the gate surrounding the runway. Mark loved to observe people and their activity. We'd sit in the car, watch the flights and talk. One evening we got out of the car and walked around the perimeter of the airport. We could feel the pressure of the wind as the planes taxied for their take off. Mark turned and hugged me, and then he kissed me.

Our relationship was moving ahead, but I still struggled with religion. I was overly concerned about the importance of how things appeared and doing certain things in the name of pleasing the Father. But in reality, it was more about pleasing people. I wore my suits and heels to church and Mark would wear his jeans and cowboy boots. He owned suits but did not believe in wearing them to church unless it was specifically required.

After a year of us dating, the traveling ministry decided to move on to another area. Mark was debating whether or not to remain in Nashville or to continue traveling with the team. We began praying about whether or not I should leave to go with him, if he chose to remain with the ministry. Ultimately, he decided that it was time for him to discontinue his travel, so he ended up staying in Nashville and the ministry went on without him. He continued to attend New Life.

Eventually, I started experiencing some insecurities about our relationship and began to take it out on Mark, not treating him the way that I should have. A gentleman, he'd open and close doors, send roses for no reason, and take me to dinner at very nice restaurants. He treated me the way that I deserved to be treated, as a daughter of the Father, but I didn't know how to receive it. I wasn't used to being treated that well. I just couldn't figure him out.

At my job the older women knew that I was dating someone seriously. Thinking they were being helpful, they'd tell me that I needed to understand after I got married, my husband was going to have "someone on the side." In my mind, I was thinking no way! He's not going to be with me and then with somebody else. I spoke to Daddy about it and he assured me that was not the case with Mark, that it wasn't his mindset. Yet and still, I couldn't wrap my mind around why this man was being so sweet to me. Sometimes I would ask him directly, and he'd say, "That's the way a man is supposed to treat a woman."

I later found out that his mother, who'd raised Mark and his brothers as a twice-divorced single mom, taught her sons to be gentlemen. Despite my mistreatment of him, Mark was a very patient man. But eventually his patience with me began to wear out.

One day, while I was in my room getting ready for one of our dates, Mom appeared in my bedroom doorway.

"Before you leave, I need to say something, Patricia," she said. Whenever Mom addressed me like that, I knew it was serious. I stopped what I was doing, sat on the bed and gave her my full attention.

"Patricia," she began. "You and Mark have been seeing each other for a while now. He is a good man. But he is not going to allow you to keep mistreating him the way you do. If you don't change your behavior toward him, you may run him away."

I knew Mom was right. Deep down I knew that I wasn't acting the way that I should. But at my young age and with my lack of experience, I didn't know how to fix it. Sure enough, it all caught up with me. Shortly after Mom's talk Mark decided that we needed to separate. We had been dating for some time and it was getting serious. He said he needed to figure out some things and I knew that I needed to, also.

A major issue that fed my insecurity was that Mark had a relationship with the Lord that I didn't understand. It's funny because when I had prayed and asked God for a husband, the number one thing on my list was that this man would love God first. I thought I knew what that meant. But after meeting Mark, I realized that I had no idea. I was with a man who would go on fasts effortlessly, and could worship and pray his way out of any situation. Even in an emergency, when it seemed as if a decision had to be made right away, he would stop to consult with the Lord first. I was with a man who truly did place God as the top priority in his life, and the truth was that I didn't know how to handle it.

After we had been separated for a few months, I dreamt that I was getting married but when I got to the altar, I couldn't see the face of my husband-to-be. I strained to see who he was, but I just couldn't make out his face. I asked the Lord what the dream meant, and the Holy Spirit told me, "I sent him, but you've rejected him." I didn't understand. Mark and I were no longer dating each other. There was another young man I had been seeing before dating Mark, but he'd long been out of the picture.

"Who, Lord?" I asked. "Who is the man you've sent?"

I sat with that question for a few more months until one day, out of the blue, Mark called. He said that he'd been doing a lot of thinking and praying, and that he wanted to us try again. I agreed and shortly thereafter, we decided to get married. At point I knew that the man at the altar in my dream was Mark. The Holy Spirit told me that I had rejected him because of my own issues. I still needed to work through that, and I was grateful to have another chance and to be marrying a godly man.

Three months before Mark and I married, I had a wonderful surprise—a daughter who I desired so much in my heart. Yes, this was my second time having a child outside of marriage. And, yes, I was full grown, I knew better, I was still a born-again believer, I read the Word of God, and I prayed in tongues. Mark and I were doing all of the above as far as serving Jesus Christ. But we had gotten very close, and that led to the conception and birth of our baby girl. I had even prayed for a daughter, but I didn't know it would happen before we got married. I'm not condoning what we did by any means. It's simply the truth. Mark and I didn't get married because of our daughter. We truly loved each other and knew it was God's plan to commit to one another. We just stepped into marital life a little early.

* * *

Several years after we were married, Mark and I were driving, and I was thinking back to when we first met.

"Mark, that night we met, sitting at the dinner table, you told me you were not going to get married unless God came and told you."

"Yes," he replied. "And He did. The Lord came while I was driving one day and told me 'Patricia is your wife.'"

"Well, you never told me that!"

"That's because I just wasn't ready to share it. You had to work through how you were feeling and acting with me, so I kept it to myself."

I never had any doubt that I was supposed to marry Mark. He'd confirmed it to me as well. But hearing that the Lord confirmed it to him made me feel really good. I also learned from Mom shortly after we'd married that she'd received a letter a from prophet whose ministry she'd been supporting. In the letter he thanked her for her offering and also said that February 12 was going to be a special day for her. That was the date that Mark and I were married.

Becoming a mom of two was an adjustment for me, but then becoming a wife was an even bigger adjustment. Learning to manage my home and take care of my husband and children was a lot of work. I was twenty-two when we were married, so I was still very young. Mark was just as supportive and loving as he'd always been. The biggest challenge for me was separating my household from my parents'.

Being the only child of older parents, they doted on me. They guided and directed me in almost everything that I did. I relied on them heavily as co-parents for David, in a way. They would take him to school and drop him off while I worked. At one point when he was really little, Daddy noticed something a bit off with his eyes. They were beginning to cross, and so he arranged for him to see a specialist who recommended a procedure to reverse the condition. Daddy paid for all of it. So, when Mark and I married it was difficult for them and for me to create the proper separation. I didn't need to rely on them as much because I now had a husband who was more than capable of taking care of me and our children. This caused some issues in my relationship with my parents and with Mark.

Six years after Marketta was born, I became pregnant with our third child, Charles. I was over the moon about that pregnancy because I wanted to have a son with Mark. Our baby was a promise from God, fulfilled. It had been prophesied to me many times that I would have another baby boy. And sure enough, after some time trying, he came.

At that time there was a strain in my relationship with my parents and even with Aunt Folia. During our disagreements Uncle Oney would not say anything. He'd just sit there with his lips pressed together tightly. It seemed as though I couldn't make a decision without one of them questioning it. I loved my family, and I know they loved me, but that was a difficult season. My husband and I were creating a new normal, building our own family and life, and I think they had a hard time settling into their new roles. I believe they took their discomfort out on me without realizing they were doing it.

My saving grace during that time was my mother-in-law, Verna Douglas. She was beautiful; she looked just like Mark and she was soft spoken. Verna worked as a sales representative for both General Mills and Mattel. She got saved in the late 1980s and became a powerhouse for the Lord. God took her to the mission field, sending her to Honduras, India and Singapore. She would hear from God and prophesy accurately. Verna and I had a Naomi and Ruth relationship and we developed a deep love and respect for one another. She was aware of the difficulties I was going through with my family and how they treated me at times.

I had gained a lot of weight from my pregnancies and I just didn't feel like going to visit family because I knew that they would talk about it. They had some kind of issue with heavyset people. During one holiday dinner the year before, Aunt Folia commented about my weight. After that, I avoided visiting my parents.

When I had Charles, Verna promised to fly down to Nashville from New York to help me. Charles was born in January, and that year Nashville had the biggest snowfall in recorded history. Verna had already told me she was going to come take care of me and help because no one else had offered. She said the Lord told her to get her ticket and fly down on

January 8. I was two weeks overdue with Charles, just as I was with my other children. When I went to the doctor, he said that they were going to schedule to induce labor on January 8—the only date they had available and the same day Verna was set to arrive.

It turns out that I had Charles on that day, as planned. I cried all night just thanking God for my blessing, my promise. The next morning, Mom and Daddy came to see me in the hospital while Mark went to the airport to pick up his mother. When my parents arrived, the first thing Daddy did was get out his checkbook and write a check for the baby. He did that for all of the kids.

Verna stayed with us that whole week. She got up with the baby at night and prepared meals for me. The next week, my family wanted to come over Mom and Daddy, Aunt Folia and Uncle Oney. Mark had to work, and he told his mother that if she were not at the house, they would not be welcome to see me. He knew about the strain and the stress it was causing me.

My family was set to arrive any minute and I was so nervous. Verna assured me that it was going to be okay. Charles was only a week old and my hormones were all over the place. My aunt and uncle really wanted to see the baby and Verna, so they all decided to come together. When they got to the house, they hugged Verna and came in and sat down. Mom told Verna that she must have hated having to fly all the way to Nashville just to take care of me. She said she was sure that Verna had other things to do. Other comments were made that were not encouraging to me at all. The whole time I was shrinking in my seat, worried about how the visit would go. Verna replied to everyone's comments.

"Let me tell you all something. It has been my utmost pleasure to serve my daughter-in-law. And if I had to do it again I would. I bathe her, I wait on her. Whatever she needs, I am happy to do it."

The response shut down any further negative talk, and I could feel myself getting more comfortable. I was grateful to have Verna there to take up for me. And I'm thankful that, over time my relationship with my family eventually was fully restored.

A few years, later I had the opportunity to return Verna's kindness. Before she was to leave for a mission trip to Singapore, Verna contacted us with some difficult news. She had been diagnosed with cancer and was scheduled to have a lengthy surgery ahead of the trip. Verna had been living in California at the time, and after the surgery she was preparing to leave on a ship that carried supplies for missionaries as they traveled around the world. Singapore was one stop on the trip that would involve many other locations.

We could not talk to her for almost a month after the surgery, but Verna had given the doctors Mark's contact information so that they could provide us with updates. Eventually, she was able to call us herself. She told us that she was not going to be able to go on the mission trip and wanted to come live with us for a while. Of course, we agreed. I made arrangements to fly out to California to get her and we flew back to Nashville together.

Verna warned me about the side-effects from her surgery so that I wouldn't be alarmed when I saw her. I'm glad she did, because when I arrived in California I was shocked. She had dark patches on her face, and her hair had thinned. She was not on chemotherapy, as the the Lord had told her not to take it. Prior to the illness and surgery her skin had a beautiful glow, and her hair was full. This was how I was used to seeing her.

After a couple of months of recuperating, Verna was well enough for us to go shopping and out to for dinner, and she had become a part of our church. I introduced her to our friends and associates; everyone who met Verna fell in love with her.

Our kids loved being around their Grandma Verna. On Friday nights she would read to them from the Chronicles of Narnia. They loved it. The kids would eat popcorn and sit at Verna's feet with great expectation as she read. She left the books to me for the kids as an inheritance.

Verna had great taste and enjoyed looking her best. She reminded me so much of Aunt Folia because she enjoyed shopping and we would often shop together. On one occasion, I took her to the boutique where I worked part-time. We had just gotten in a beautiful black wool cape trimmed in a leopard print.

"Oh, Patricia, you have to buy that," Verna said.

"It's too much," I quickly replied, alluding to the style. I knew it would draw attention and I was still dealing with shyness and fear of people, so I resisted it.

"Try it on anyway," she insisted. "And try on that hat and buy that, too."

I did as she advised, and they looked great. After a few turns and twirls in the full-length mirror, I became more comfortable. I began to feel like the "real" me. So, I bought both items, and I still have them today. Twenty-five years later they are as fashionable as they were when I first bought them, and I always receive compliments when I wear them. Wearing the hat and cape make me feel fabulous, and most importantly, they are a representation of Verna.

Some of our friends would take Verna to dinner and pay to get her hair and nails done. We all enjoyed each other and had a great time together. Verna was a tremendous cook. One day she decided to make homemade spaghetti sauce. We went to the store to pick up the ingredients. Nothing she purchased came from a can. It took eight hours just to cook the sauce. The house was filled with such a wonderful aroma. I can smell it now.

After about a year of Verna staying with us, the Lord told me to stop working at the boutique. I didn't know why, but obeyed what He said. A month later Verna fell ill again, but this time she didn't bounce back. I knew then that I would be taking care of her, and that is exactly what I did.

Being a caretaker for my "Naomi" was a learning experience. Serving in that role was new to me. And even though she was unwell, we enjoyed every moment together. Unfortunately, around this time my relationship with Mom became more strained. It was somewhat tense before then, but now it had worsened. I sensed the changing dynamic between us causing a divide between me and Verna. Verna recognized it and told me to not let it bother me. She encouraged me to continue to respecting Mom's role as my mother, even though she was beginning to mistreat me.

I was grateful to have Verna during this time. I cleaved to her because I needed her love. We didn't always see eye to eye, but she was not manipulative like I felt my mother was starting to be. I understand that control and manipulation come from fear. Especially if a person feels they are losing one they love to someone else.

Mom's behavior towards me created tension in our relationship for almost 30 years. That may be hard to understand, given how the Father eventually restored us, but that restoration came at a steep price. We were caught in a severe spiritual battle. On one hand, God was using her to impart spiritual truths and revelation to me, but on the other, the enemy was coming between us and began to take over her moods and actions. At first, I didn't understand what was going on. I couldn't see that a demonic spirit was at work. I later learned that other people saw it but didn't tell me.

By the time Mark and I moved into our first house in the mid-1980s, the strife had risen up in a major way. I had become afraid of my mother. I never wanted to do anything to upset her, so I walked on eggshells around her. Mom could be loving one minute, and then without warning she'd become controlling and manipulative. She would have what I called "spiritual temper tantrums", where one moment she was fine, and the next she would have a complete meltdown.

As the years went by, the Lord began to show me how to manage these situations with Mom. He'd tell me to pray before I called or went over to visit. Daddy served as a buffer between us for many years.

* * *

After a few months of taking care of Verna, the Lord prompted me to accompany our pastor to a conference in West Virginia. Verna encouraged me to go, so I did. While driving to the conference I began to weep uncontrollably, and I knew that the Lord was letting me know He was preparing to call Verna home. Once we arrived at the hotel and got settled, I shared with my pastor what the Lord had told me. That night I dreamt Verna had died, but realized it was a tormenting dream intended to keep me from the assignment with my pastor. I remained in prayer regarding the Father's revelation the entire time that I was away. When I returned and walked into the house Verna was there to greet me.

"There's my sunshine," she called out. She was lying on the couch, so I sat on the floor next to her.

"Did the Lord tell you anything about me while you were in West Virginia?" Her question caught me off guard. I knew that she had an intimate relationship with the Lord, but I was still surprised.

"No...He didn't," I quickly replied, denying what I knew to be true.

"Are you sure?" she pressed me. I looked down.

"I don't remember," I said. Then, realizing it was possible that she knew what He'd told me, I continued. "Verna, I could be wrong, and if so, I don't want you to be angry," I said softly.

"Sweetie, I won't be angry," she replied. "What did the Lord say to you?"

"He told me that He's calling you home," I confessed. Tears started to well up in my eyes. I looked over at her, and she was beaming. She appeared to be elated to hear what I'd said. "You know?" I asked her.

"Yes, Sweetie. I love you—all of you—very much, but I'm ready to see my Lord and King," she said. She was practically glowing. Then she asked me a question I never expected to hear. "Would you release me?" she asked quietly.

Verna had embraced our Naomi and Ruth relationship as much as I had. I treasured it. She was my advocate, friend, confidant and a second mother to me. She had been my rock during some very difficult times, and I still wanted her to be with me.

"I can't release you, Verna, please don't ask me that," I said.

"It's okay honey, I won't be angry," she said softly. "I understand how you feel, but I'm ready to go."

This ended the conversation for the time being. But I refused to accept what she'd said. Eventually, Verna again asked me the question—if I would release her—and I needed to give her an answer. It took a while for me to respond.

The next day went by, and I didn't say anything. I prayed to Father God, and I went back and forth in my mind. Was I really ready to let her go? I knew she was waiting for me to respond. By the third day I realized that she was becoming uncomfortable I could tell that she was in more pain. With the Holy Spirit's help, I told her that I would release her to the Father. Five days later Verna entered into Glory. My Naomi was gone.

Reflection

It's time for some real talk. As I mentioned in an earlier chapter, I got saved at twelve years old, adopted into the family of God. Shortly thereafter I received the baptism of the Holy Spirit with the evidence of speaking in tongues. At that time all I knew was I am not going to hell, which back then was most important in a religious setting. God's plan for having my parents adopt me, and for Him to bring me into His spiritual family shaped more aspects of my life than just salvation and being baptized in the Holy Ghost. It led me to meet the love of my life, my husband, who was a man of God.

Becoming one with my husband also meant what was mine was his, and what was his was mine. In that, I inherited my beautiful soul of a mother-in-law, whom I believe God sent to cover me and love me through some of my most vulnerable moments. When I could not rely on my parents, aunt and uncle—the only family I'd known up until that point—God brought Verna to sustain me.

Jeremiah 1:5 says that God knew us before we were formed in our mother's womb. Isaiah 46:10 says that Father God knows the end from the beginning. He knows everything that we need, even every person that we need, to help shift us from one dimension to another. Even when the families He plants us in do not show up for us in the way that they ought to, when they fall short of His glory, Father God yet makes provision for us. These are the kingdom benefits that we receive as adoptees into God's family. We have assurances that even though there may be times that we are down, we are never counted out.

CHAPTER EIGHT

Uprooting Seeds of Silence

I believe every person has something that they want to change about themselves. Everyone has things about themselves that they do not like or feel as if they have no control over. For me, it was my shyness and discomfort around people that had developed as a young teenager, and that by my twenties had grown into overwhelming fear. I recognize now that is what it was: a spirit of fear and paranoia.

I was constantly concerned about what others thought about me and how they viewed me. Some would call it "people pleasing" and I think that's right. I cared about what people thought so much that it would cripple me. If I walked into a room and people turned to glance at me, which is normal behavior, I'd interpret their looks as criticism. I'd go home at night and be unable to sleep, thinking about a person and what they said or what they were "really" thinking about me.

Daddy would often have to encourage me, saying that people were not thinking about me at all. While I was worrying about what they'd said, they had gone on about their business. Mark said the same thing as Daddy and they did their best to bring me to reality, but I couldn't believe or receive what either of them were saying. My emotions were always upside down.

Internally, this fear caused me to fret all of the time. Externally, it manifested itself as silence. Fear literally bound my tongue. It stole my voice and suppressed my opinions. Instead of walking with my head held high in confidence, I would shrink back. In the midst of worrying about what people thought, I would cry out, *"No!"* on the inside. I wanted to speak up for myself. I wanted to show who I really was, but fear held me in a firm grip.

When I was around six or seven years old, I remember Mom describing me to people as shy. That went on for many years. I was not assertive, and I wouldn't look people in the eye when I met them. I would stand at Mom's side, clinging to her skirt. Of course, Mom didn't realize it at the time, but calling me shy from an early age planted a seed. She said that I was shy, so I began to believe I was shy.

I think that when people have beliefs that are contrary to their identity in Christ, they know deep down something is wrong, even when they can't put their finger on it. Saying that you are shy essentially is saying that you are afraid. I know that now. I think growing up sheltered by my parents contributed to that. I wasn't allowed to go many places or participate in activities other kids did. I didn't interact with a whole lot of people outside of my family. I was kept close, near home. My parents did the best they could to raise me well and to protect me. Maybe it was in that sheltering that my shyness developed.

Even after Mark and I married I continued to be shy, and I was very sensitive to what was said about me. People would say things out of pure innocence, and I would get upset. On the other hand, people might take advantage of my being shy and say something inappropriate. I would get angry in in those cases but couldn't bring myself to say anything in response. I wanted to speak up, but it literally felt as if something would well up in my throat to keep me from talking. If I didn't try to say something in reply my response usually was to cry. There were other times when I would see people and want to strike up a conversation but wouldn't have the nerve to do it. It was a miserable time in my life. But I thank God for my husband. He was consistently loving, gentle and patient with me. He showed me the love of the Father, and I believe that early on he chose to see me for what I would become in Christ instead of what he saw in me at that time.

The Father was faithful. He surrounded me with people like my husband, and women who were a little older and more mature than I was, who could be examples to me.

In my mid-twenties I had a friend, Mary who ran a catering business. We met at New Life, where Mark and I had met years earlier. Mary and I would go out to eat, and if her food had not been made to the specifications that she'd given to the server, she'd send it back—every time. I would never do that. Even if my order had not been prepared to my satisfaction, I'd accept it and eat it anyway. Once, when we went out to eat, embarrassed after she'd sent her meal back yet again, I tried to convince Mary that it wasn't that serious, that she shouldn't always send her food back. She looked me directly in the eye and said, "Trish, I'm paying for my meal, so I have a right to have it prepared just the way that I want." That settled it. And besides, she was right.

Around the same time, Mary introduced me to a woman named Ms. Margaret. She was very savvy in business, but also regarding things of the world, and she was spirit-filled. She owned a beauty salon and designer boutique, and the Lord would lead me to her shop on Saturdays. Out of obedience I visited for several weeks. I would just sit quietly and observe while she worked on her clients. I witnessed how strong and confident her voice was when she spoke. I could see how she wouldn't tolerate certain things—not because she was older, but because she valued and respected herself. Over time I joined in the conversations she had with the ladies, and began to find my voice and become more confident in engaging with other people. Ms. Margaret was always encouraging me.

She never referred to me as shy. I think she knew that I was someone who was withdrawn and needed time and space to open up.

Between these two women, who became dear friends, and the encouragement of my husband, the Lord gradually began to break fear off of my life. This process took years, with many steps forward and a few steps back.

Mark and I had begun to minister in worship at churches in the area. We would sing and break up the fallow ground so that whomever was set to minister the Word could just come in and preach. At the time, I was perfectly content with our ministry as worshippers. But Mark saw more. Either his heart was so strong toward God, and there was much that the Father was telling him, or he just knew by revelation. He knew that there was a mantle over our lives to preach the Gospel, and he shared it with me, but gently, because I think he knew that I wasn't in a space to completely receive what he was saying. He said that we will have a choice to obey or not. It was difficult for me to hear because I was at a point where I still couldn't talk to people in the way that I wanted. I would shut him down, but he continued to lovingly and gently cultivate me during those years.

I remember once a woman with whom I sang in Nashville's city choir attended a service where Mark and I were preparing to minister in song. I saw her walk in just as we were getting ready to sing and I immediately shrank back. Mark could sense that I didn't want to sing with her there. She was an amazing singer and as far as I was concerned, no one in the area could out-sing her. I was afraid of being judged or compared to her. In one of the few times that Mark expressed frustration with my timidity, without saying a word, he let me know that he didn't care who was in the audience, we were going forth to minister. He grabbed my hand, pulled me along, and we went on to sing.

I was contending with fear, instead faith according to Jude 1:3, which says, "Beloved, when I gave all diligence to write unto you of the common salvation, it was needful for me to write unto you, and exhort you that ye should earnestly contend for the faith which was once delivered unto the saints."

The Father sent prophets to Mark and I that spoke the Word of the Lord over our lives. The words we received confirmed what the Father had been telling him for years. I always envisioned Mark one day leading a ministry with me supporting him from the back. I saw myself as a first lady, wearing a big hat and suit of course, and carrying his Bible. My role would be to just handle whatever he needed me to do personally to help him minister. The fear totally blocked my vision so that I couldn't see clearly. But little by little with Mark ministering to me, and the word of the Lord ministering to me through others, the Father made it clear that my destiny involved ministering alongside my husband—not behind him.

People would at times prophesy the great things that Mark was going to do in ministry. And then they'd say, "your wife is going to have to catch up." He didn't like when people said that because he knew how it would shake my confidence. While he knew that they were well-intentioned, all I could hear was that I wasn't good enough or was lacking in some way. I didn't believe it was possible for me "catch up" to Mark.

Once when, we were ministering at a local church, we were asked to sing the duets, "I've Just Seen Jesus" and "More Than Wonderful" by Larnell Harris and Sandy Patty. The service was being held in a school auditorium in downtown Nashville. We were led through a side door to enter the building and remained backstage until it was time for us to minister. We were cued to move on stage, behind the closed curtains. When they opened, the place was filled. There had to be about 2,000 people, the largest crowd we'd ever ministered to. I was terrified. But we stepped forward, and as usual, Mark held my hand and we began. Once I got started flowing with the Holy Spirit the glory of the Lord fell upon the room. We received a standing ovation. God got all of the glory out of that experience.

Shortly after that we met a couple who was moving to an Indian reservation to do missionary work, and attended a service with them to minister in worship. At the end of the service a prophet who was in attendance approached Mark and I and said that he had a word for us.

"Man of God, you will be healing people with your shadow, just as Peter did in the time of the early church," he said. The prophet added there were things that Mark would have to obey and do before those things took place. I began to weep, which was not uncommon. The Spirit of God would come over me and I would just cry. Then prophet turned to me and said,

"Oh, Little Jeremiah, my crying prophet."

This was the first time anyone had referred to me as a prophet. It was hard for me to receive, but it was affirming to be associated with Jeremiah, the prophet who would give a word to the people, and feeling God's burden for them so deeply, he would cry.

"I'm not doing this anymore, they are not listening," Jeremiah said. But then he couldn't resist prophesying, as in Jeremiah 20:9: "Then I said, I will not make mention him, nor speak any more in his name. But his word was in mine heart as a burning fire shut up in my bones, and I was weary with forbearing and I could not stay." He had to keep going. After that encounter, I cried for almost two hours. When we got home, I called my best friend, Rosalind, and she asked how the service went. I told her it was okay, and then shared what the prophet had told me.

"Patricia!" she responded. "You have to understand that is what God has called you to. There is more to you and Mark than singing anyway. There's a preacher in you. Darlin' it's going to be so good."

She had told me that the real me is bold and outgoing, and that I only needed to accept that about myself. I would try to argue with her, telling her that I didn't have anything to say, and she'd reject it outright. I had plenty to say, she said, I was just subdued, and that she thought it related to my upbringing. Shortly after that conversation, as we continued to go out and minister, I finally began to see what Mark had known and seen all of this time. There was more for us to do than worship and sing. I began to receive more prophetic words and revelation from the Lord that my "shyness" was likely connected to my being adopted, to generational issues and to ungodly soul ties. Rosalind confirmed this by saying that since Mom was kind of shy, and I picked up more of that from her than Daddy's outgoing personality.

The Father was beginning to call us to preach. It was the early 1980s, and we knew that we also were called to be pastors, but we went through many years of ministering, studying, and praying about things that God had spoken to us personally. It was as if we were going through the school of the prophets according to the Old Testament. God would direct us to do things, and we'd do them, just like David was anointed King while he kept sheep and then served under Saul. The Lord confirmed to me personally that He was calling me to preach the gospel, and he called Mark and I old-time prophets, like Ezekiel. Finally, God told me specifically that I was a prophet, but I never told anyone other than my husband. And he, of course, already knew. As time went on and we continued to minister, I would operate as a prophet in the various houses where we were invited, but there was only one time that I identified myself in that way.

During this time, I continued to be delivered from my shyness. I desired to be free, meet people, speak to strangers. I wanted to reach out but was still too afraid, dreaming of the day when I would be free to be the real me. I said to myself, *"One day, I'm going to be able to meet people. I won't be shy anymore. I'll be able to articulate. Someday I'm going to get up, walk to the podium, look out to the audience and preach with boldness and not experience any fear."* I could see it—the dream that the Lord had placed in my heart. Gradually, as I cried out and began to renounce fear, He was setting me free.

One day I was walking into a department store. I went through the glass doors and as I passed someone, I said, "Good morning, how are you today?" They responded. I went on about my day and they went on about theirs. It didn't occur to me until a few days later, what I had done. I had actually initiated speaking to someone. I didn't wait to be spoken to or avert my eyes to avoid having to say anything, like I normally did. I actually opened my mouth first. At that moment, I realized that something was happening in me. As time went on, with the help of the Holy Spirit, I was coming out of fear and bondage. I was being released to fully become who God designed me to be.

Soon after, I began to speak up more in conversations. I shared my opinions. At work, I'd enter the break room and look around to see who was there to speak to. I would start conversations, and when people spoke to me, I engaged with them. I no longer looked down or to the side. It took time for me to become comfortable with it. There were times when I spoke up, and other times when I still held things in. I also dealt with not trusting people, based on how I was sometimes treated when walking in fear. It wasn't always balanced. But the Lord was faithful to me as I was faithful in moving ahead.

Over the years, I continued to receive words from people, confirming God's call on my life and on Mark's and my ministry. Mark was hosting an evening service at the church we were attending at the time. A woman of God who was a prophet and very accurate began to attend and shared the word of the Lord. She prophesied things that years later have come to pass. She would tell us that the Lord would wake her up in the middle of the night and teach her. One evening after choir rehearsal, she pulled me aside.

"Now, Pat, you're gonna have to come on up," she said. You and Mark are gonna be pastors together."

Some years later, we were attending service at our church. A man from South Africa asked if he could minister to me. My husband and I agreed, and he told me that I was getting ready to blossom. He said the real you is getting ready to come forth.

God began to speak to me even more. He ministered Ezekiel 3:9 to me, which says, "I will make your forehead like the hardest stone, harder than flint. Do not be afraid of them or terrified by them, though they are a rebellious people." Just as the Father had told Ezekiel, He told me that only if I don't say what He tells me to say, that I will be shamed. He revealed to me that I had to set my face as flint because the enemy will try to use things to distract me. I could not look at people's faces as an indication of whether or not what I was preaching was resonating with them. I had to move ahead with confidence in Him. With the Father's help and that of my husband, that's exactly what I did.

Reflection

God wants to manifest Himself through people he sends to us. In this chapter I discussed women that God placed in my path to speak life into me. Proverbs 27:17 says, "As iron sharpens iron, so a man sharpens the countenance of his friend." These women had to challenge some of the traits and characteristics I picked up through the nurturing of my adoptive parents. These were things that were contrary to who Father God was calling me to be and calling me to do. They were calling me into a realm that I would enter into soon. The Lord also used complete strangers to confirm His words to me.

I didn't exactly laugh in these women's faces, but I behaved like Abraham's wife in Genesis 18:12-13, "Therefore Sarah laughed within herself, saying, after I am waxed old shall I have pleasure, my lord being old also?" Sarah laughed because she could not believe or receive what the Lord was telling her He was going to do. Like Sarah, I chuckled many times about the things the Lord was saying about me.

God is patient. I believe He also wants us get understanding, because He does not make mistakes. The Lord would not tell us to do anything that would harm us. It may harm our flesh, meaning that we have to crucify that flesh. He has a plan and destination for each of us, and He will send His anointed with messages to remind us. I encouraged myself in this journey by praying this scripture: "And when he putteth forth his own sheep, he goeth before them, and the sheep follow him: they know his voice. And a stranger will they not follow, but will flee from him: for they not the voice of strangers," (John 10:4-5).

Mom and Marketta (1983)

Mark and me on our
Wedding Day (1983)

Mark and me worshipping (2016)

Ministering at
"A Few of My Friends"
(2018)

CHAPTER NINE

Answering the Call

Years before it actually took place, Mark heard from the Lord about our call to pastor. This was consistent with how we usually received instructions from the Father about something significant for the both of us and our family. Mark hears it first, and then me. Depending on the circumstances I will either be in full agreement right away or take some time to get on board. This time though, somehow, I knew deep inside that we were called. In my heart, I said, *"Okay, Lord, have your way with us."* But my thoughts were not wrapping around the idea very well. I think it was largely due to the fear that continued to pursue me. Although I'd found my voice, the Lord was still in the process of completely freeing me. And Mark and I were still serving within our church and being strengthened in our areas of gifting. So, it was ten years between the time we heard the call to start our church, and the time that we actually moved in faith to do it.

Mark and I were ordained pastors for about thirteen years before we started our church and began walking in that office. Mark was actually ordained twice. He was ordained in 1993 at a church we attended when we lived in Georgia. They did not ordain me because they didn't believe in women preachers. They just said I would be an evangelist, and Mark would be ordained.

Then, in 1995, we were ordained in Nashville. Although I had earlier received the words about me blossoming and catching up to Mark to minister, I still was not putting together the vision to pastor or preach. I couldn't see it. We were invited to preach here and there, but we didn't do anything in terms of pursuing the call to pastor.

For many years Mark and I remained hidden, growing in the Lord, serving and raising our family. While there wasn't much happening in the natural to indicate where the Lord was taking us, spiritually, the Father was speaking to us. There were things of the kingdom He was revealing—especially to Mark. I believe he knew that eventually we would do something together, but neither of us knew what that would look like.

After our ordination, we just thought it meant that we could preach officially, and we didn't think a whole lot of it beyond that. We also kept singing, and soon came to realize that the Lord would use that gift to open up opportunities for us to minister, beyond worship. Sometimes we'd minister in song and then begin to speak prophetically, but that didn't always happen. If God said to go, we'd go, and if He'd say share, we'd share.

Over the years, more and more people began to confirm the prophetic words I'd received about launching out alongside Mark. They were seeing what was in me and spoke what they saw. In 2003, when I was working at Nordstrom in the makeup department, my Aunt Folia's comment to Mom many years earlier, about my having an interest in and eye for fashion, had come to fruition. I was untrained, literally taught by the Holy Spirit, but among the best makeup artists working at the store at that time.

One day while at work, I noticed a striking woman striding toward the counter. She moved as if she were gliding across the floor. She had fiery, red hair and wore a long, tailored green dress. I was drawn to her and knew the clerk working at the counter, so I went over to say hello. The red-headed woman turned to look at me. We locked eyes and she said,

"The enemy is trying to do a spiritual hysterectomy on you. He is trying to take all of the creativity that is in your womb."

I just stood there and stared at her. She continued, "You feel that just when you think you're going to move up or into a new realm, the Lord says no, not just yet. But one day, he's going to release you to take off. You feel as if you're on a cabinet shelf and the door opens and you're not picked up just yet."

I didn't know this woman from a can of paint. But I knew by the Holy Spirit that she'd heard from the Lord. I took what she said to heart and never forgot it. It turns out that the creativity that she spoke about was exactly what the Father wanted my husband and I to use as we prepared to launch our ministry a few years later.

By then we had been living in Atlanta for nearly ten years and were members at our local church. Our church was one of the largest in the area. I was feeling settled there and thought we would stay for the long haul. Despite the size of the congregation we were able to connect with the people who, today, are part of our covenant sphere of influence.

Mark and I were very active, and I thought that eventually the senior pastor would release us into ministry under the church's umbrella. It was common for ministers who were active and had a call to plant churches or launch ministries to do so with the church's blessing, and essentially under the church's name. Mark and I knew what God had called us to and I thought that we would be released in that manner. Proverbs 16:9 says, "A man plans his way in his heart, but it is the Lord who determines his steps."

And so, it happened that one Sunday Mark was on his way to church and heard from the Lord. We sometimes drove separately because he was part of the praise and worship team and had to arrive early for sound check. After the second service, Mark and I met in the parking lot and he told me we needed to talk later that evening. It sounded serious. I couldn't imagine what he wanted to discuss. That night he told me that something had happened to him while he was driving to church.

"I was praying about Nashville and the issues there and began to ask the Lord what He was going to do about it," Mark began. "The Lord said that there was a lot deliverance and healing to be done there. I agreed and told Him that He needed to send someone there to serve the people. The Lord agreed with me. Sweetheart, in the next second I realized what the Father was placing on my heart."

Mark paused. I stared at him and nodded my head slightly as if to say, "go on."

"Honey, I asked the Father, are you going to send me back? And He responded by asking if I would go."

Mark paused again. I was frozen to my seat. I could not move. My heart was beating so fast and I couldn't feel myself breathing.

"I told the Father that I would move back on one condition—yes I gave the Lord a condition. I told him that I've got to have a pastor's heart. That's the only way I can do it."

Mark fixed his eyes on mine. "Honey, the Lord said, *I can do that, Mark.* I cried all the way to church because I knew what that would mean for us—and for our family."

After Mark finished, I exhaled loudly.

With my heart still beating fast, I launched into problem-solving mode. We lived in Atlanta, and Nashville was about four hours away. There had to be a way to make this work.

"Okay, Sweetie," I started. "Okay. So, what we're going to do is have church on Saturdays and then come back to our church to serve on Sunday."

"No," Mark replied quietly.

"Okay then... What we'll do is have church early Sunday morning in Nashville and get on the road back to Atlanta..."

"Honey," he said. "You're not understanding me."

"Well, what am I not getting?"

"We're going to move back to Nashville and start a ministry."

I knew my husband. So, I knew God had spoken to him. Many people had spoken words similar to this over the years. I would say, "Mark, people are saying that the Lord said..."

His response would always be that he didn't care what they have to say, and that he's not doing anything until he hears from the Lord himself.

I was in agreement with what Mark had just shared with me. The only thing that I told him was to hurry up and make plans to do what the Lord is saying, because I didn't want to enter into disobedience. That comes at a steep price that I was not willing to pay. He assured me that the Lord said we cannot go until 2006, which was the following year. One reason was that our youngest, Charles, had to graduate from high school, and Marketta was pregnant with our first grandchild, who was due around the same time. I was so excited, nervous and overwhelmed all at the same time.

A few weeks later, I drove up to Nashville for a short visit and to share the news with my parents.

"Mom and Daddy, I have to tell you something," I said. "We're coming back to Nashville to start a church."

Mom was excited. She lifted her hands and the first thing she said, and I know it came from the Holy Spirit, was "I've been praying that God would send a church here that's on fire for Him." During my visit I realized my family was in need of a caregiver; all five of them were elderly and needed additional support. My short visit with them ended up lasting nine months. I called Mark to tell him what I noticed when I arrived in Nashville and we both knew something had to be done. So, we would communicate via phone and pray for Godly wisdom, for family, ministry and the entire transition. Everything was about to change. I would return home on some weekends to check on Mark and the kids.

Mark and I had been praying about what the Lord wanted us to name our ministry. While I was back in Atlanta one weekend, we had a chance to talk. I told him that I kept hearing two words in prayer: "Covenant" and "World." He said that he had been hearing identical words. As we continued to pray that weekend, the Lord made the name clear to both of us. World Covenant Church International. I traveled back to Nashville with even more excitement about what the Lord was doing.

In May 2006 I returned to Atlanta. I had a peace from God, and Charles our youngest son was graduating from high school. I dared not miss that. My parents drove down with me to attend the commencement. After all the festivities were over we sat down again with Charles to let him know the time was coming close for us to move. He was eighteen and had decided that he did not want to go back to Nashville.

I wasn't completely comfortable with it, but the Lord shared some things with me that gave me peace. Marketta was living on her own and, she, too, desired to remain in Atlanta. In July she gave birth to our first grandchild, Jada. As a step of faith, on the last Sunday of that month Mark and I drove up to Nashville for our first Sunday service; we returned to Atlanta afterward. We did it one other time in August, and through prayer, at the end of the month, Mark felt that I should go ahead and get things started with our Nashville ministry and continue to care for my elderly family. So in September, I left Atlanta and headed to Nashville, leaving behind our youngest son, first grandbaby and daughter.

When I returned to Nashville, my family seemed to be doing somewhat better. One of the first things the Lord told me to do for our ministry was to begin having prayer and Wednesday night Bible study. About a month later we transitioned to having Sunday service as well. Ms. Margaret, had told me the year before that if I ever needed a place to pray, I could use her salon. I hadn't shared any of the words we'd received over the years about ministering, but I had told her we were returning to Nashville, and I knew that the Holy Spirit was bearing witness with her about what we were doing.

We started praying every Monday at the salon, and it continued for three years. Mark remained in Georgia seven months after I had left for Nashville to get things started. Now we were praying about when he would leave Atlanta to join me.

God began to answer and give confirmation, Mark moved back to Nashville in February 2007. By this time Mom and Daddy had become a part of the ministry. Daddy took the role of our treasurer, but he could also pray. Mom was the silent intercessor. As the Holy Spirit led at times Mom would give a prophetic word or speak in tongues with interpretation. Even though Mom had joined our ministry with Daddy, and we had some really good patches, the strain between she and I continued.

Mark and I had heard clearly from the Lord and followed his instructions for launching our ministry. But it wasn't too long before opposition came from the outside. Whenever you move out into the things of God, especially if they are to have a significant impact on your life or the lives of others, the enemy is bound to use people or circumstances to frustrate your progress.

For the next year, that is exactly what Mark and I faced. When people found out about our ministry, and especially the name, we were told "you're only supposed to use 'international' if you're actually doing international ministry."

Mark would reply gently, "It's World Covenant Church International. You are welcome to join us."

I would say, "Well, I think we're just doing this by faith, we believe the ministry will be international." And that's how we handled it.

Mark was determined to move ahead as he and I saw fit, but hearing some of the comments from others, I sought ways to make sure our ministry appeared legitimate to other people. I began researching and making calls to learn how we could potentially obtain information or endorsements from our earlier associations in Atlanta. We visited Atlanta again and met with people Mark knew through working in ministry. They were happy to be of service to us by basically giving us a whole laundry list of "dos" and "don'ts"—rules that we needed to follow to make sure our church was structured properly. As we listened, we realized that we didn't have in place most of the things that they had advised us to have;

nor did we have the people and finances to make all of them happen.

I began to get nervous and then intimidated. When we returned Nashville, I paced the floor. I prayed and told God that we were told that if we don't meet certain requirements, we couldn't be part of their network. I believed that to move forward we needed the support and experience of our former ministry. We'd never done anything like this before. I called Mark at work.

"Mark," I began. "They said that if we don't check off this list, we can't be part of their network," I said.

"And?" he said.

"But Mark, they said that we can't move this forward without having a board and all of these other things in place."

"I know what they said, honey," he said. "And I don't care. What is God telling us to do?"

Mark was right. God told us that we were to start a church, World Covenant Church International. There were so many people in our ear during that season, giving their advice on what we should or shouldn't do, how we should or shouldn't be going about things that I admit, I was distracted by it for a while. It became overwhelming. That old religious mindset came back, so that the only way I could see successfully building a church was the way that I'd seen it done before. If there were a model, why did we need to reinvent the wheel? I'll tell you why. Our ministry was completely going to be of the Lord. Mom encouraged me to think about it in that way. When I told her that we would have to get certain things before we could start, and that our church would have to be established under a larger ministry. She simply asked me, "Why?"

I realized that when the early church started the Apostle Paul didn't have all of the structures, and leadership tiers, and red tape to build, disciple and encourage the church. He didn't have a larger ministry overseeing what he did. He didn't have an abundance of finances or people he could trust. What he did have was the commissioning of God the Father, the headship of Jesus Christ and the indwelling Holy Spirit. And guess what? Mark and I had the very same things. I almost allowed my issues to stop us from doing what the Father was calling us to do. I thought that because we didn't have everything that most other ministries had in place we couldn't move forward. I was willing to use it as an excuse to be disobedient. But the reality was that the Lord told us to go to Nashville and start a church. That was it. So ultimately that's what we did.

As we became even more determined to move ahead, the enemy turned up the heat. People were saying things about us and our ministry. Things such as, they're not a "real" church, or they're out of order, practicing heresy, and they're rebellious. And all of that because we would not follow man's ideas or man's path.

Potential members would desire to join our ministry, only to be told that we were wrong. But because they had heard from the Lord, they stayed with us. The words still hurt me, but Mark couldn't care less. One Sunday after service, a young member of the ministry told us that she had been told we were out of order. It bothered me so badly, it hurt me. I thought, *Oh God, why would they say that? We didn't do anything wrong.*

The following day, I was on the phone praying with the young woman. I felt so wounded. The next thing that I knew, the power of Holy Spirit came upon me. I slid off of my couch and hit the floor. I lifted my hands. The Lord said to my spirit so clearly, *"You are not going that way!"* Just like that. The path that I'd tried to follow is not World Covenant's path. The validation that I was seeking was not part of God's plan for us.

After that, I never said anything else about it. But every now and then I'd get that itch. As we've gone along and seen other ministries that are growing, I'd begin to think that it's because maybe we're not a member of a larger ministry. In my heart, I did not want to be like Israel begging for a king when God didn't want them to have one. He desired to be their King. I truly wanted what God wanted for us and the ministry.

The following year a church associated with our former church in Atlanta was having a special service, and the Lord told Mark and I to attend. So, we went every night and sat in the back. During the last night as the final service was wrapping, it was as if the Holy Spirit had shifted some things. The Word of the Lord began to flow from some of the same people who had said negative things regarding World Covenant. Mark and I watched in awe as words of knowledge and prophecy flowed with accuracy concerning us. We smiled. We had already made the decision that we were going to walk in love, I just had to get over the rejection we'd experienced from people, especially when we were just being obedient.

It paid to obey the Lord and to go to these meetings. We received vindication, but not by our own hand. It was the Lord's. In the years since, we occasionally attend events our former ministry hosts and each time they greet us warmly.

* * *

On October 14, 2010 my daddy became our first member who transitioned to Glory. The Lord had been telling me for a while he was calling Daddy home. I had just returned from ministering at my first women's conference in Utah a month earlier. I had no idea that my daddy would soon be gone. The Sunday before he went into the hospital, he was at church testifying about God's goodness. He even said some things to the congregation about how he loved and appreciated me and how I had helped him and Mom.

The next day I received the call that Daddy wasn't well and had been sent to the hospital via ambulance. I was scheduled to take him to physical therapy the next day. When I arrived at the hospital that Monday evening, I asked him what he was doing there? He smiled, but he was in pain. He had been through a lot.

Daddy had an illness that occurred over the years; this was something the Lord had graced him to walk in for a long time. But it now was taking a toll. Mark had asked him some years earlier whether he was ready to go home to be with the Lord, to which Daddy answered, "Yes, son, I'm making myself ready." Mark requested that Daddy stay until his first great-grandchild was born in July so that he could bless her. Daddy replied that he'd pray about it and see what the Lord said. Well, he came back and said that the Lord said he could stay a little longer, which turned into four more years. His transition affected us all, but we knew he was one of those that Hebrews 12:1 speaks about, "A great cloud of witnesses".

After Daddy's passing, the tension between me and Mom became the worst it had ever been. She blamed me for his death and told everyone in the family that I was responsible. For peace of mind I had to back away from her. I knew I needed to help her grieve and assist with settling Daddy's estate, but I couldn't do it. In that time of weakness, a distant family member and even strangers stepped in and began to take advantage of Mom financially. They corroborated the negative things that she said about me and cashed in while they could.

Marketta eventually moved to Nashville to help. While this was going on, I stepped in to help with Aunt Folia and Uncle Oney because they were ailing. That was incredibly difficult as Mom began accusing me of trying to take over their house and money. She would get into these fits when she'd call me seven or eight times back to back in the wee hours of the morning and she'd holler and threaten me. By this time, my Aunt and Uncle had to move to an assisted living facility. After one year in the facility, when I thought things couldn't get any worse, Uncle Oney passed away.

A year and a half later, mom had to move into a facility herself. I was able to place her with Aunt Folia, so the sisters were together. In 2014, Mom became very ill and because the prognosis wasn't good, we didn't think she would make it. She wouldn't eat, talk or move and she was frighteningly thin and pale. She had gotten so sick that we were told to arrange for hospice care. During that time, I stayed at her side almost every day and night, praying and talking to the Lord. I knew that was not the time for her to leave, but I couldn't put all of the pieces together.

Sure enough, after a few months, Mom did what she usually does and bounced back to health. When she was healed from her illness, our relationship began the uphill climb of being restored. It was then that I adopted the name Sweet Pea for my dear Mom.

A few years later as I was getting ready to shower one day, the Lord talked to me and told me about two services where I would minister. Then He said, *you've wondered about your mom. She has imparted a lot into you, just like your dad. From her, you received prophetic gifting. From your Dad, you received a mantle to preach the gospel and to pastor. The reason that you went through such a spiritual battle with your mother was because the enemy was trying to prevent that impartation from happening.*

The Father had told me that if the enemy could stop me from receiving what he had for me, he would. I knew what I'd received from Daddy. Many years earlier, before he died, I had a dream where he hugged me and said I'm placing my mantle upon you. Now, it seemed as if everyone had slowly began making their heavenly transitions. This included Aunt Folia, my second mom. In July 2016 my aunt said "see y'all later" for the last time. At ninety-seven years old she went on to Glory.

* * *

Today, World Covenant Church International continues to chart its own path. God told us that we were not to build a tent in Nashville, but that we were designed to plant and go. Our ministry was founded to make disciples in all nations. We teach people about God and His Word, how to live daily, and how to hear his voice. We show them that while there is validity and a need for the five-fold ministry, the promises and inheritance of God is for the body of Christ. We pastor more people who are not members of our church than we do our actual members. Our desire is to train them up and send them out for the upbuilding of the Kingdom and to the Glory of God.

The Father has expanded our ministry to include Mark and Patricia Douglas Ministries, where we travel evangelizing and discipling the nations and ministering through television. For the past two years, I have hosted "A Few of My Friends", a women's ministry designed to help uncover the hidden treasures of darkness, and riches of secret places that God has placed in women. We bring health, healing, deliverance, restoration and nurturing through the Word of God, to help women reach their maximum potential in the Kingdom of God. In line with God's mandate for us, we provide training, teaching, impartation and make disciples.

Reflection

Psalm 32:8-9 TPT, says:

I hear the Lord saying, "I will stay close to you,
instructing and guiding you along the pathway for your
life.

I will advise you along the way
and lead you forth with my eyes as your guide.
So don't make it difficult; don't be stubborn
when I take you where you've not been before.
Don't make me tug you and pull you along.
Just come with me!"

There is nothing wrong with admiring someone else's work whether in business or ministry, but the path that the Lord has laid out for you will be different. Don't get stuck trying to make God fit into a mold, especially with regard to ministry. Proverbs 14:12 says, "There is a way that seems right to a man, but its end is the way of death."

Not choosing God's way or His plan will always cause unnecessary hardship. You may not have a manual written by someone else on how to do what God has told you to do. But you will have the BEST guide—in the person of the Holy Spirit. One thing to remember about being adopted into the Body of Christ is that we all have a unique call. Remember God chose you for a special purpose. He has need of the gift He placed in you to build up and edify His family.

EPILOGUE

A Sweet Pea Legacy

As I write this final chapter, I am relaxing in Orange Beach, Alabama with Mark. He has taken me away for eight days of rest, after the death of Mom, my Sweet Pea. I had not expected my sweetheart to transition during this time. It has been a time of grieving and mourning for me as well as my children. My Sweet Pea played a big part in all of our lives, and I have known her for nearly my entire life. Her departure was quick. In our eyes, it happened suddenly. The Lord had been preparing me for about ten years, but this year He began to speak to me more about her leaving. When the physical transition actually took place, still we all were shocked. And honestly, I'm still in shock today. It hasn't even been a month that she's been gone.

We all have heard the saying "this too shall pass." As I look across the Gulf Shore, the water's movement is creating a beautiful white foam. I hear the endless sound of water. At night the heavy tides bring the water in close to the beach condo where we are staying. The ocean's edges lap at the shore. God has been so faithful to me. Mark and I have stepped aside for these few days to position ourselves to hear from the Lord, and minister to Father God even here on the beach. We've been out this morning since about 10 o'clock. It is now after 1 p.m. We love it here. Every morning I am up and ready to go the beach. I tell my husband "you are moving like a turtle." His response? "And you are acting like a kid at Christmas."

I give praise to God and I thank Him so much for my Mom. I know where she is now, and I know she's rejoicing. It's where she always wanted to be. I'm reminded of the time back in April when my daughter, granddaughters and I went to Centennial Park in Nashville for a quick outing. Since we could not schedule in-person visits due to COVID-19 restrictions, we scheduled a 2:00 p.m. FaceTime call with Mom. When we finally connected, she was rejoicing, crying and worshiping Father God. She kept saying, "I know that I'm saved, born-again and I know I'm going to be with the Lord. I'm so excited!" When I shared this with my husband later that day, he told me then that she was preparing for her transition.

Little did I know that just three months later, July 28, 2020, would be the day that the Lord would call her home. He had given me a word of knowledge back in May, when I had to select a new facility for her. The Lord said, *"Whatever you choose, it will be fine because it will be temporary. I'll call her home to be with me, and I'll take care of her forever because she longs for me."*

I even said to Mom after her transition, "Well Momma, are you thinking about me at all?" I know that might seem selfish. And it's not that I didn't think she should be excited about being in the presence of the Lord, worshipping at His throne. However, I have to admit that I had this thought more than once. "Mom, do you know that you left me?"

Maybe these are normal questions people ask when someone so dear to them passes away. I don't know. While we were traveling to Orange Beach, my husband asked me, "Honey, do you think you're grieving so much because of your Mom? Or because of your whole family?" I had to really think about that. Because I never really grieved for my whole family after taking care of them for so many years. The transitions began in 2008 and then continued in 2010, 2012, 2016 and now 2020. Aunt Pat, Daddy, Uncle Oney, Aunt Folia and now Mom.

Even earlier today on the beach I thought about the word that a prophet gave me on a cruise Mark and I took last year. This woman of God was so accurate about my life, where I was then, and even where I was going. It was one of those "meaty" words from God. Anyway, the Lord said through her, "You were not just sent to this earth to take care of your family." Wow! That stung a little bit. Because I really thought that one of my missions in life was to be a caretaker. After all, I was the only child and the only niece. For whatever reason I thought that God had purposed it that way, so that I would take responsibility for them as they began to get older.

Now they are all in Glory. There is no one to check up on, no one to go see in the hospital, or visit in assisted living. There is no one to talk to via phone or, with the emergence of COVID-19, to connect with by "touching hands" through a window. The lack of physical interaction due to the coronavirus made it even more difficult to deal with mom's transition. Not being able to touch or hug her, not being able to hold her hand or be with her when she transitioned was extremely hard. Marketta still hasn't gotten over that. However, my last physical contact with my mom was a kiss on her forehead as she laid beautifully in her casket. This is what I always did when I would go visit her, give her a kiss on the forehead. In turn she would kiss me on my cheek. I did have time with her and held her hand at the chapel the day of her visitation. That's where I kissed her forehead for the last time. Of course, there couldn't be a kiss on the cheek for me.

Months earlier, as the pandemic unfolded, I remember thinking to myself *I don't know what I would do if mom was to leave at this time.* People were forced to do drive-by visitations and funerals. Can you imagine? Though Mom did end up passing on during this time, we were able to have a visitation with a limited amount of people and social distancing. I cannot even begin to express my gratitude for the response to her transition—the gifts, cards, calls and texts.

* * *

Mom went to the hospital on July 23 and I had two meetings that day. The one in the afternoon was very important. At 11:30 that morning I received a call from Mom's facility. She was being taken to the hospital by ambulance because they believed she had double pneumonia. I called my husband and then Barbara, who met me at the hospital. We found out it was more serious than they expected, and according to hospital rules we could not see her. Once Mom was admitted there was nothing I could do. They didn't want visitors sitting in the lobby, so we had to leave. The nurses took down my phone number and said they would call to keep me updated. So, I kept my meeting that afternoon. As I drove to my meeting, I prayed in the Spirit and then burst into tears. I screamed in the car, "Lord, have I not done all I could for her?"

When I arrived at the office for my meeting the young lady asked me if I was okay. I shared with her what was going on. While in the meeting, the young woman shared some news that I could not believe. We were meeting about something completely different, however, this topic came up literally out of nowhere. It was wonderful news, something that had been in the making for years, but I was not able to comprehend it at that moment. My response to the Lord was, *"Now? Now Lord? How could the blessing I'd been awaiting manifest at a time when I wasn't in a place to fully receive it?"*

A few days later, we spoke with the doctor about Mom. He explained that her condition was okay at that moment. But within twenty four hours of that conversation she'd declined. I received a call from the palliative nurse, and I knew what was next—hospice. The hospital had done all they could, and now Mom needed to be made comfortable. I never wanted my Sweet Pea to suffer, so I agreed to whatever measures were best for her. Marketta and I went to meet with the hospice representative. I couldn't think straight, but we made all of the necessary plans, and had a chance to speak to mom very briefly. We told her that we loved her. To have the chance to do this was the favor of God, and even then we knew it.

On July 28, I went to Walmart to pick up some things. I didn't feel right. I had very little strength. When I returned home, the hospice nursed called me to let me know that she had just visited Mom. We discussed doing a FaceTime call with her and Mom when she returned for her shift the next day. Unfortunately, that never happened. Within an hour of us hanging up the phone, the charge nurse at the hospital called me and said the words I never wanted to hear.

"Is this Patricia Douglas?" she asked gently.

"Yes, it is," I replied, knowing what she would say next.

"Ms. Douglas your sweet mother has passed away." I had no words. I held the phone. I was with my daughter and oldest granddaughter, Jada, and they both heard what she said.

"Ms. Douglas are you there?" she said. I asked her to repeat what she said again. I didn't know what to say. I couldn't think. I told the nurse I had to go. Marketta got up and immediately went outside to call her brothers. Jada began to cry, and I consoled her. Then I got up and went back to the bedroom and laid on the floor. I cried and screamed until I was heaving. I called my husband and Barbara. All I could do is scream, "She's gone, she's gone, she's gone!"

When I finally came to myself, I heard Marketta on the phone starting to make arrangements with the funeral home. I came back into the room where we had been sitting as she continued to talk to the funeral director. I laid on the couch to rest. I was completely numb. I was trying to wrap my head around the entire day. Everything you could possibly imagine was coming through my mind. The last time we saw Mom, which was the day before, she was beautiful. I remembered how she smiled. We told her we loved her, and I could tell she was trying to tell me the same thing, but she was having issues breathing being connected to the oxygen equipment. But she looked gorgeous.

Once all the arrangements were made, my husband and I

decided to stay in a hotel in Nashville until everything was over, to avoid having to drive back and forth from Murfreesboro. My emotions were everywhere. I did pray. I called on the Lord and prayed in the Spirit. He was all I had. The celebration and gravesite service were powerful. The Holy Spirit's presence was weighty. My mom was remembered by those who eulogized her as a general in the gospel, a prayer warror and intercessor—even though she never had a platform. We laughed and cried as we reflected on memories of Mom.

I miss her so much, and yet reflecting on my Sweet Pea I can see that she imparted so much into me spiritually. I carry so much of her within me. Mom is one of the main reasons this book was written. Some adoptions are not ideal. Children are often mishandled or mismatched with families. But my adoption was godly from the beginning. It was ordained by Him, there's no doubt in my heart. I carry the mantle of my Daddy and Mom, and for this I am so grateful. Philippians 1:6 says, "Being confident of this very thing, that he which had begun a good work in you will perform it until the day of Jesus Christ."

Thank you, Leslie and Dahlia Parker, for choosing me by the prompting of Holy Spirit to be your daughter. Thank you, Father God, for orchestrating such a wonderful connection and placing me with them. And thank you for adopting me, Father, as your beloved daughter.

PRAYER OF SALVATION

Father God in heaven, I know you love me and always have even when I didn't recognize you. But now, I am recognizing you as God. I believe Jesus Christ is your only begotten son, and that he died and was resurrected. I'm ready to receive Him in my life. Forgive me of my sins in Jesus' name.

NOTES

1. "adoption." Merriam-Webster.com. 2020. https://www.merriam-webster.com (November 2020).

2. A. A. Allen, "About Us," aaallenonline.com, accessed February 5, 2020, http://aaallenonline.com/about-us/.

3. Nashville Woolworth's, "History" woolworthonfifth.com, Accessed May 19, 2020, https://woolworthonfifth.com/history/.

CPSIA information can be obtained
at www.ICGtesting.com
Printed in the USA
LVHW082044200221
679530LV00012B/201

9 780578 823164